WINNERS ~~NEVER~~ *ALWAYS* QUIT

Seven Pretty Good Habits You Can Swap for Really Great Results

LEE J. COLAN, PH.D. AND DAVID COTTRELL

ALWAYS
WINNERS ~~NEVER~~ QUIT
Seven Pretty Good Habits You Can Swap for Really Great Results

Printed in the United States of America
ISBN: 978-0-9819242-3-6

Credits
Developmental editor: Jeff Morris
Contributing editor: Alice Adams
Proofreader: Deborah Costenbader
Cover design: Melissa Monogue
Text design: Jeff Morris

Dedication

To everyone who has ever quit
something good so they could
stick to something great.

CONTENTS

● Introduction: Don't Quit Yet!. 7

1 Quit Taking a Ride . . . and Take the Wheel 13

2 Quit Getting Comfortable . . . and Explore the Edge 23

3 Quit Analyzing . . . and Follow Your Intuition 33

4 Quit Managing Your Time . . . and Manage Your Attention . . 43

5 Quit Showing Interest . . . and Commit. 53

6 Quit Moving . . . and Be Still 63

7 Quit Striving for Success . . . and Seek Significance 73

● Epilogue: Never Quit Quitting!. 81

● Winning Tips Summary. 85

Don't Quit Yet!

One day as Lucas was passing by the office of one of his most loyal, trusted team leaders, he overheard her say, "I just wish he would quit doing that."

He stopped, ashamed of eavesdropping on one end of a telephone conversation but unable to move.

Behind the half-open door, Kristen went on. "I wish he would quit over-thinking things. He has good instincts, and he ought to follow them more instead of beating a problem to death. I love working for him and I'll always go to bat for him, but we could get way out in front of the competition if he would sometimes just go with his gut!"

Quietly, Lucas went on his way.

He sat in his office, shaken. He thought about what his top engineer had said.

What was it she wished he would quit? Thinking? Thinking too much? Not relying enough on his intuition, his "gut"? Did she mean he was being too analytical?

Maybe Kristen was right. Maybe he needed to rely more on how he felt about things. But how could he shut off his own rationality?

Lucas was by inclination and by training a rational leader. He prided himself on his ability to rise above the personal conflicts that often swirled around major decisions, to reason dispassionately with his managers and cut through the irrelevant side issues to the logical core of the matter. Disciplined rationality gave him control. Even now, sitting at his desk, he was reasoning with himself, using his rational mind to quash the inner turmoil he was feeling. Yes, perhaps she was right. Perhaps he did need to rely more on his gut.

But why was he so bothered by what he had overheard? It was simply the opinion of a trusted subordinate, an opinion that he knew had some truth in it. And it was given—even if it was behind his back—in a benevolent spirit and without harshness or any intention of undercutting him.

He respected Kristen's judgment too much to shrug it off. Was it true? Was he doing too much thinking and not enough acting? Was he holding his company back? That possibility was reasonable, worth thinking about. But why should it have shaken him so?

Then it came to him. It was the word "quit" that had jumped up and slapped him in the face. There was something about that word. . . .

● ● ●

Seven-year-old Lucas had struck out for the third time that afternoon. Frustrated and embarrassed, he picked up his baseball bat and glove and walked off the diamond and out of the ball park.

"Quitter! Quitter! Dugout sitter!" jeered the other kids, his teammates too, as he tearfully ran toward home. The taunts rang in his ears even after he was out of earshot.

Lucas picked at his dinner that evening, saying nothing. Up in his room, he lay on his bed, staring at the wall. After a while, his father climbed the stairs and sat on the edge of the bed. Gently he coaxed the story out of Lucas. They were both quiet for a minute. Then his father spoke.

"Son, it's just not a good idea to quit. Like my dad said to me when I was about your age, 'Son, quitters never win.' What he was telling me was that there's one sure way to lose, and that's to quit. So don't ever quit. Just give it your best and keep going."

And so it was that Lucas inherited the legacy that had been passed down from his father's father and from untold generations before.

As he continued through life, Lucas found himself following his father's admonition to the letter, long after the humiliation of that day on the sandlot had faded from his thoughts. Whatever the project, he never gave up. His high school football team, his college major, his first and current job, a project, a relationship—he always hung in, even when the going got tough. His perseverance was one of the traits that had helped him become a successful executive, a leader in his industry.

● ● ●

Quit. The word rang like an alarm bell.

He had simply overreacted to that word, that humiliating word from his boyhood. Is that all it was? Well, he wasn't a kid any longer. And he never quit anything. He had learned how to hang in there when the going got tough. He could get past the word. It was just a word . . . or was it?

Was there really something he needed to quit doing? Was there a time to persevere and a time to quit? Could quitting lead to better things?

The more he thought about it, he could see that "quit" was not necessarily a negative word. You could quit a bad habit, quit a bad situation, quit a strategy that's not working.

He smiled. He could see the light of reason here. Quitting could be healthy. Maybe he should get better at quitting.

● ● ●

Lucas is not very different from the rest of us. Just like Lucas, we all navigate our way through the course of every day by force of habit. Most of our actions are built-in behaviors, instilled by natural inclination and the weight of experience.

Patterned behavior helps us function. We use what we've learned, what we've been taught, what has worked before. It lets us get the job done without concentrating on every action, and it usually keeps us out of trouble. Not having to plan our every move, every second of every day, is an enormous time saver. We brush our teeth without thinking about it, use turn signals subconsciously, cook dinner while listening to the news.

But there are exceptions. We all have behaviors that are detrimental. Many are trivial, like compulsively interjecting "uh" or "you know" into our conversation or turning on the TV even when we know there's nothing on worth watching. Others are dangerous, like smoking or speeding. Or smoking *and* speeding (a person of our acquaintance nearly drove into a ditch when his cigar ash fell into his lap).

We resolve to do better, especially around January 1 of each year. And each year, for the most part, we fail to mend our ways. Our natural tendency is to avoid change unless it's absolutely necessary. Just keep doing the same thing and everything will work out. After all, who do you know who enjoys change? Change is like rain; we all know it's good for us, but we don't like to get wet. There's even a popular book whose title sums up the prevailing attitude: *Change Is Good . . . You Go First!*

Yes, change is good for everyone but us.

Things are not going quite right, but we convince ourselves that to quit doing one thing and begin doing something else could make things worse. It feels safer, more comfortable, to keep doing the same old thing rather than doing something else that might lead to better results. It's like the old vaudeville routine:

> Patient: It hurts when I do this.

> Doctor: Then quit doing that.

Quitting is required for success when, in order to do the right thing, you have to quit doing the wrong thing. To quit is to change, and change is tough, because our fear of things getting worse naturally overshadows our hope of improving the situation. We focus on potential disadvantages, even when we know success hinges on change.

● ● ●

Quitting isn't for sissies. It takes guts, and quitting well requires care and forethought. You can't just quit and hope for the best. Why?

- ● **Things change!** In our information-rich, time-critical world with its ever-changing options, we have to constantly reconsider whether we're adding value to our lives or just clutter. If something is draining our energy, can we do without it? Does a crammed schedule help us achieve our goals? Maybe it's time to quit doing some things and instead do other things that help us go where we want to go. There's a wealth of information available to help us decide.

- **Priorities shift!** Our personal and professional situations demand that we make changes. Career priorities, project priorities, family priorities, personal priorities, social priorities—they all shift over time, and sometimes on a moment's notice a budget gets cut, a former pet project is put on the back burner, a spouse gets transferred.

- **Timing is everything!** There's a time to persevere and a time to quit. Time doesn't care who we are or how we use it to achieve our goals; it treats us all equally and without mercy. Deciding when to quit and when to stick with it depends more on your current circumstances and options than on what you've done in the past. The important questions are: What are you doing now? What do you need to be doing now? What do you need to quit doing now in order to be doing what you need to be doing now?

● ● ●

Perhaps we caught your eye and your interest with our title; now you've learned the kind of thinking that's behind it. You can see that we want to challenge your assumptions, stimulate your creative mind, and provide simple tools to help you build winning habits.

And it's not as though we're standing in the pulpit and preaching to you. No, we're as guilty as you are. Think of us as sitting at the table with you, sharing the lessons we've learned ourselves by making mistakes—the same things you may be doing today without a second thought. Things that are perhaps holding you back, keeping you from winning.

We all know too well how ingrained practices can sink any project axle-deep in well-worn ruts. Whether you lead a team at work, at home, or in the community, this book will help you examine not only your own habits but those of your team. Each chapter ends with action points that you can both (1) apply to your own practices and (2) use as discussion points with your team.

There are no neutral decisions in life—every choice either does or does not get us closer to our goals. If we say no to something that's not a high priority, we're saying yes to what we have deemed more important at that time. When it comes to our time and energy—our precious resources—we must choose carefully when to quit and when to persevere.

This book will show you that quitters actually do win—but only those who are selective and thoughtful about what they're quitting. We'll discuss seven pretty good habits you can swap for really great habits—and really great results!

Fasten your seatbelts! Ready? Now, start quitting—and get ready to win!

David Cottrell   Lee J. Colan

The way to get started is to quit talking and begin doing.

—Walt Disney

QUIT TAKING A RIDE . . .
AND TAKE THE WHEEL

Be the change you want to see in the world.

—Mahatma Gandhi

Gretchen Butterworth was the kind of person, people said, who attracted bad luck the way honey attracts flies. And it was such a shame, they said, because she deserved better. A kinder, more generous person you wouldn't find.

Gretchen lived on her meager social security benefits. Since her husband had died, she had looked for ways to stay active and involved in her community, and perhaps earn a little extra money so she wouldn't have to live on soup and sandwiches at the end of every month.

She did volunteer work down at the town library, but when a position opened up for an assistant to the head librarian, although Gretchen was highly qualified, a young man with an English Literature degree was hired. He moved into his spacious office and soon began to demonstrate how little he knew about libraries and about getting along with other workers. Gretchen was disappointed but just smiled and went about her work as usual—in addition to covering up the new employee's mistakes.

ALWAYS

(handwritten correction over "NEVER")

She decided to rent out a room in her house for extra income. She advertised for a single woman and soon found a tenant who seemed to be ideal. Within a few weeks, though, the young woman's boyfriend was spending the night, and not long after that had moved in all his clothes and a stereo that blared all night. When his car materialized in her driveway, blocking access to her garage, Gretchen sighed and parked in the street. She didn't want to raise a ruckus.

Gretchen often complained about her problems when her friend Candy came by the library. Candy offered sympathy and gentle advice. "Did you apply for that position?" she asked. Gretchen told her no, that she had thought it would be obvious she was qualified. Candy shook her head and smiled. "Sometimes you have to speak up, Gretchen."

Those who let things happen usually lose to those who make things happen.

—Dave Weinbaum

Candy was not afraid to speak up, but it had not always been so. She had not spoken up when her first car had turned out to be a lemon or when she learned that her husband had been cheating on her. But when her husband's lawyer had tried to convince her it would be better not to ask for so much child support, she got her own lawyer and persuaded the judge to award her the house, the car, and a hefty trust fund for the kids. That was how she learned it was sometimes wise to speak up.

Since her divorce, Candy had put her son, her daughter, and herself through college, started a successful catering business, and become one of the town's most admired business owners. She had a reputation as a tough negotiator, always driving a hard bargain, but always with a smile. If a client cancelled at the last minute, Candy kept the deposit; if it was an emergency, she gave it back. She devoted much of her free time to volunteer efforts and gave generously. Everybody liked her, and nobody tried to take advantage of her—at least, not twice.

What made the difference? Gretchen and Candy came from similar backgrounds, encountered similar difficulties, but where Gretchen accepted defeat and kept her pain to herself, Candy fought back.

What it boiled down to was this: Gretchen allowed herself to be a victim; Candy did not.

A victim is a person to whom life happens. A victim is a passenger in a runaway car, waiting to see which ditch the car will end up in today and wondering if she will come out of it alive once more.

Candy didn't see the point of letting the car drive her. Instead, she instinctively slid in behind the steering wheel and took control. After many years of practice, it was as natural to her as breathing.

Gretchen never felt herself in control. She didn't complain much, but when she did, it was about her inconsiderate tenant, her unsympathetic supervisor, her chronic bad luck. It wasn't so much that Gretchen chose to be a victim; it was simply a habit.

Candy didn't complain at all. When a difficult situation arose, she simply worked through it and overcame it. Even when she lost a client, she quickly found two new ones who were better. She had learned long ago how to turn lemons into lemonade, and it had become so ingrained in her that the concept of bad luck never entered her mind.

Candy didn't wait for life to happen to her. She dealt with whatever came her way, turned problems into opportunities, made things happen that would move her ahead. For people like Candy, the sky's the limit.

RIDE OR DRIVE?

On any of life's journeys, we have to make a choice before we begin the trip. Our options are these: we can be a passenger, or we can be the driver. It's our choice.

People who choose to be passengers have to go where the driver is going. Passengers have no control over how fast they move ahead, no say about whether rules are observed.

Then again, being a passenger has its appeal. You can just sit in the car and relax, oblivious to your final destination. You can plug in your earbuds and listen to music, or you can nap. You can text a friend on

your cell phone or do sudoku puzzles. You don't have to pay attention to where you are, who's in front of you, who's behind you, or whether you're making progress. Your journey may be pleasant enough, but if you choose to be a passenger, you're just going along for the ride.

It's not what happens to us but how we choose to respond to what happens that determines our next move, next path, next relationship, and next risk. If you choose to be a driver, you accept the responsibility for moving toward your goal. You pay attention and focus on getting to your destination. You make decisions on how quickly to move ahead. You avoid potholes and stray ice chests in the road. You decide when to stop and refuel. You may choose to take a detour. You make all the decisions that affect the safety of your passengers and your success in reaching the goal.

The physical distance between a passenger and a driver is less than three feet; the psychological distance is enormous. Which would you choose to be?

EXPECT THE UNEXPECTED

When things are going the way they're expected to go, most people feel they are in control of their lives. This is an illusion. In the larger sense, you can't control all the events life throws at you, or even most of them. The only thing you can really control is how you respond to them.

When the unexpected happens, the illusion of control can vanish like your kids at dishwashing time. People react to the unexpected in one of two ways. Some take the role of the victim: "Wasn't my fault. Nobody could have foreseen it. Nothing I could have done about it." This is a "passenger" reaction.

Others see an opportunity to truly take control: "Okay, things have changed. Let's see what we can do about it. Maybe there's a great opportunity here." This is the way a "driver" reacts.

A real driver has the remarkable ability to deal successfully with the unexpected, the unusual, the extraordinary. Positively dealing with the unexpected by looking for solutions, not excuses, is the choice winners make.

If you know someone who is masterful at dealing with the unexpected, take a closer look at that individual, because you've truly met a special person.

Jim Lawton is like that—he is a driver. Whatever comes his way, Jim can handle it. His dad died while Jim was a freshman in college, and as tuition money dwindled, Jim found enough work to support himself and stay in school.

Don't dwell on what went wrong. Instead, focus on what to do next. Spend your energies on moving forward toward finding the answer.
—Denis Waitley

After graduating, Jim went to work for a company that eventually had to downsize. When that happened, Jim networked his way into a new company and a new job. No, not a "better job," just an ordinary job, but he mined every opportunity that came his way, and he kept moving ahead.

Jim hasn't allowed anything to keep him from being successful, no matter what life has tossed his way. He chooses to avoid becoming a victim of life's circumstances. He has made up his mind to deal with the unexpected.

Jim knows there's no grand conspiracy to make life hard for him. He knows it's not what happens to him, but rather his response to what happens, that makes the difference. Today, Jim is within reach of his personal and professional goals when others, with fewer obstacles to overcome, have failed to accomplish theirs.

Believe it or not, the unexpected is going to happen. It's your choice how you deal with it. You can be a victim, or you can choose to realize that you can make strides toward greater success by taking control of the unexpected.

Do we sometimes fall into the victim trap? Of course. Occasionally feeling sorry for ourselves is natural, but remaining in the victim trap will keep you from achieving success.

ALWAYS

Avoiding the victim trap is not easy, but it's a choice you have to make. You control your next move. Will you sit and sulk, or will you commit to continuing toward your ultimate goal?

FOCUS ON SOLUTIONS

When problems arise, what's your first reaction? Do you think like a cop, identifying culprits and assigning blame? Do you vent your anger on anyone within your yelling radius? Do you submerge yourself in regret, thinking, If only? Or do you immediately get creative and think, How can we make this right?

Lee: Early in my career, I asked my boss why, when the rest of us couldn't find daylight, he could see the light at the end of the tunnel and it was always coming from a rainbow?

"It comes from a lesson I learned long ago," he said. "The more you focus on the positive side of life, the more you will attract the positives. The things we focus on create a magnet for our lives."

As the years since then have taught me, my boss was right. Focus on excuses, and every challenge is a stumbling block. Focus on solutions, and every challenge becomes a stepping stone.

During one of Franklin D. Roosevelt's election campaigns, his campaign manager was about to print 3 million copies of the candidate's acceptance speech with his photograph alongside. Then someone pointed out that the photographer had never given permission to use the photograph. According to the copyright laws at that time, you could be fined a dollar per copy for publishing unauthorized photographs. The campaign couldn't take a $3 million hit.

The campaign manager felt a tinge of panic, but instead of thinking up excuses or finding someone to blame, he kept his cool and started considering ways to handle the situation. Could this disaster be turned into a dividend? He had an idea.

He cabled the photographer: "I have a plan that could mean a great deal of publicity for you. What's it worth to you if I use your photo on this campaign material?" The photographer cabled back: "I can't afford more than $250."

It was a deal!

By focusing on finding a solution, FDR's campaign manager was not only able to prevent great embarrassment and fines, but he also forged a lasting relationship between the photographer and FDR's administration—and he got a pretty good deal for a crucial photo.

Winners are skilled at seeing solutions. They do this in various ways. One powerful way is to cultivate a heightened awareness of solutions— that is, when they encounter a problem, they immediately start seeing possible solutions. It's a habit that can be cultivated, and it has to do

---

Check Your Focus

Have you ever wondered why some people seem to have all the luck? Why some people are always in the driver's seat? In general, "drivers" elicit the best from themselves and others by focusing on

Forgiveness	vs.	Anger
Others	vs.	Self
Opportunities	vs.	Problems
Gratitude	vs.	Envy
Abundance	vs.	Scarcity
Today	vs.	Yesterday
Building up	vs.	Breaking down
Humor	vs.	Drama
Controllable things	vs.	Uncontrollable things
Giving	vs.	Taking

The more you focus on the positive side of life, the more you will attract these things. Focus on forgiveness, and you will find the world forgiving. Focus on humor, and your life will be full of laughs. Focus on drama, and your life will be a soap opera.

The truth is that being lucky doesn't have much to do with luck at all. Winners create their own luck by constantly checking their focus. They appear lucky because their focus has put them in the right place to make good things happen. In other words, luck is 90 percent preparation and 10 percent opportunity.

ALWAYS

with a take-charge mindset—taking the wheel instead of letting events drive themselves.

When we change the way we look at things, things change the way they look. If we remain open to new experiences, we discover new ways of doing things, new ways of enjoying life. If we train ourselves to think in terms of solutions instead of problems, we begin to see more solutions. Soon problems become merely occasions to find solutions—a kind of game that challenges you to solve puzzles.

You can train yourself to look for good outcomes by becoming aware of how you react when a problem arises. Do you get angry? Do you start assigning blame? If so, catch yourself before you speak. Take a breather. Remain calm. You're inside the problem; where's the exit? What needs to be done right away? What can be done later? What can be done to keep this from happening in the future?

Next time you hop into your car, consider how much bigger your windshield is than your rear view mirror. There's a reason for this: in driving, as in life, you need to keep your attention focused forward more than backward. Keep your eyes on the road ahead, always looking for winning solutions. Leave the problems and excuses in your rearview mirror.

Life's rewards go to those who let their actions rise above their excuses.
—Unknown

TAKE THE WHEEL: WINNING TIPS

- Plan for the unexpected.

  o Write down three things that, however unlikely, could adversely affect a current project or goal.

  _____

  _____

  _____

  o For each of the unexpected events you listed, write down some ways you might respond. It's not what happens to you, but how you choose to handle it, that makes you a winner.

  _____

  _____

  _____

- Whenever you see a problem, resist assigning blame; instead:

  o Brainstorm as many potential solutions as you can before you evaluate any of them.

  o Challenge yourself (and others) to find the best solution.

QUIT GETTING COMFORTABLE . . . AND EXPLORE THE EDGE

If we don't change, we don't grow. If we don't grow, we aren't really living.

—Gail Sheehy

We recently ran into a friend who, while not exactly a technophobe, would never be mistaken for an early adopter. He ignored us at first. He had a new smartphone and was busily thumbing the keys. We sat down beside him and tried to annoy him by staring.

"Yeah," he said, "I finally broke down and got a smartphone. And yes, it was for the email.

"Like I told you a hundred times, I hated the idea. I liked the simplicity of my old cell phone, and email wasn't a problem because I always have my laptop with me. I was aware of the advantages, but it didn't seem worth the hassle to change.

"I had to use the computer a lot because I travel every week and some of my clients get pretty nervous if I don't answer their emails within 10 seconds. I kept my laptop in sleep mode most of the time so I had instant access. Usually I could find a place to plug it in so the battery wouldn't run down.

"Yes, it was a pain in the butt to have to haul out my laptop in a crowded auditorium or an airport lounge without tables. I couldn't email on a plane, and there's still a lot of places without wi-fi, so I was spending a lot of time looking for electricity and a strong signal. I also got tired of having to unpack my laptop for airport security even on short trips.

"But the thing that sent me over the edge was a long drive through several western states. I spent five nights in small towns where none of the motels had broadband access. I had to struggle for hours with my dial-up modem, and it kept dropping out on me halfway through downloading an attachment.

"After struggling with it for two hours one night, I told myself it was time to join the twenty-first century.

"Right away I fell in love with how easy and convenient it was to check my email. I stopped hauling my laptop along every trip. I became more productive.

"In two weeks—well, two days, really—I got over my reluctance and became a total smartphone freak. I still can't figure out why it took me so long to wise up."

OUT OF THE BOX

Our friend had grown comfortable with using his laptop for emailing, even when it caused him problems. It wasn't that he was averse to improvement, it was just that a cell phone that could do email represented too big a break from what he was accustomed to. In his mind, he downplayed the advantages of changing and magnified his reasons for staying with the status quo. It took a major problem to get him out of his comfort zone and into a new place where he could discover all the wonders of a mobile multimedia telephone.

We are all averse to change to some degree. When things are going well, we're reluctant to upset the routine, and with good reason—"If it ain't broke, don't fix it." Even in a trivial matter, such as the route we take when we drive to a friend's house or the way we stack dishes in the dishwasher, and even if there's a good reason to try something new, we tend to keep doing what we're accustomed to. We stick with what's worked because it works. If we changed, we might realize some benefit, but typically we weigh the chance of improvement against our comfort with the old ways and find it wanting.

Every adversity, every failure, every heartache carries with it the seed of an equal or greater benefit.

—Napoleon Hill

Our friend's resistance to receiving email on his phone was disproportionate to the degree of change required. As it turned out, his new phone's technology was a huge improvement over the old way he had been clinging to. It's the same story with most changes we finally make.

Areas that are most significant to us, and where we have established our most comfortable and successful patterns, might seem to hold the greatest danger when a change is contemplated. Yet such areas are where the greatest potential benefits may lie, waiting to be discovered.

In order to grow in wisdom and spirit, we need to challenge our assumptions now and then. Even if today's challenge doesn't compel us to change those assumptions or lead us to a better answer, tomorrow's might, and the simple act of challenging ourselves brings growth.

THE PITFALLS OF COMFORT

Comfort certainly has its advantages—our comfy chair in the living room, a comfortable routine at work, a comfortable relationship. With all the advantages of comfort, here are some things you should know about the comfort zone before you explore the edge.

The comfort zone is where most of life is played. It is certainly where most of sports is played. Consider a football field: 90 percent of the game is played between the 20-yard lines. That's why they call anything outside that area the "red zone"—it's where the difference in the game is made. It's okay to feel good and play well inside the comfort zone before you explore the edge and go for the score.

But staying in the comfort zone too long can get boring. We get soft and unfocused; we don't have to be as sharp. If we make our comfort zone as big as our life, we not only lose our edge, we can even lose sight of the edge. We must ignite our own sense of adventure if we want to see what the world has to offer us and what we have to offer the world.

It's pretty safe in the comfort zone. We know the boundaries, the landscape, and the other comfortable players in the comfort zone. There is little or no risk; a misstep here or there is not very costly. But like the football team that's trapped between the 20-yard lines, we cannot win in the comfort zone. Because the risk is small, so is the reward. Learning and growth occur when we are uncomfortable. Think of the defining moments of learning and growth in your life. Were you hanging out in your comfort zone? No, you were hanging over the edge.

If you put yourself in a position where you have to stretch outside your comfort zone, then you are forced to expand your consciousness.
—Les Brown

So, in case you're hesitating to explore the edge, here are four comforting questions to help you move forward.

1. Who else has done it? You may think you're in unexplored territory, but it's unlikely that you're trying something no one else has ever tried. Look around to find others who have explored the same edge that you might be anxious about. Whether your comfort zone ends at the edge of learning a new skill, speaking in public, making a financial investment, expressing your feelings, or quitting a bad habit, someone else has been at that very same edge. That person can help support you, prepare you, and encourage you to win.

2. Can I dip my toe in first? No one says you have to hurl yourself headlong into every new endeavor. Try it out first. Start small. When you reflect on the first time you tried anything new (leading, speaking, rock climbing, painting, playing a musical instrument), you probably remember how uncomfortable you felt. But you stepped out and did it, and you soon discovered that it wasn't as hard as you had expected, right? After a while, what was once the edge became your comfort zone as you built your competence—and competence builds confidence.

3. How bad can it be? Often, the fear in your mind paints a darker picture of things outside your comfort zone than is really the case. Remember, the victory is in the exploration itself more than the success of your attempt. Thomas Edison said, "Genius? Nothing! Sticking to it is the genius. I've failed my way to success."

4. How great can it be? Your dreams are usually bigger than your comfort zone. You must be so passionate about your dream that, instead of feeling that you have to leave your comfort zone, you are magnetically drawn to the edge.

THE SLEEP OF SUCCESS

Success naturally makes us comfortable. We want to enjoy our achievements, so we tend to slack off ever so slightly, let our focus slip, play it safe. We might not notice this in ourselves, but it's easy to see in others, especially in the world of sports. How many times have we watched teams take a lead, lose their momentum, then lose the game because instead of playing to win they begin playing not to lose? They get ahead, then they get nervous about protecting their lead, so they pull back and start playing more cautiously, losing the intensity that earned them the lead. Before long, their lead evaporates.

The same is true of our own teams—success traps us all. As we exceed expectations and hit our targets, our focus subtly shifts from gaining momentum to sustaining momentum, and—whoa, what happened to all that momentum?

In business, the cost of not changing has much bigger implications than just simply changing from a cell phone to a smartphone. The stakes are high. Those who cling to the past are quickly left right there—in the past. Those who seize the moment to change are catapulted into a brighter future.

When you're competing in business, just as in sports, don't worry so much about those you're outcompeting; instead, keep an eye on those who may outcompete you. Yes, you may be comfortable doing what's necessary to beat out lesser rivals, but winners learn how to change and improve by watching the competitors that make them sweat.

Let's Get Uncomfortable

Here are a few steps we can take to transform those uncomfortable moments of change into defining moments of growth.

Take comfort in your discomfort. Recognize that discomfort is not lethal; it can be a sign of growth, a signal that changes are happening, changes that can benefit you in the long run. This does not mean that you have to be uncomfortable to make beneficial changes; nor does it mean that all discomfort is a good sign. However, if you are undertaking changes that you have reason to believe will lead to improvements, look on discomfort as a good sign. People who have learned about the benefits of constant improvement often view discomfort with a degree of pleasure; it means they are on the right track. Paradoxically, they can relax and take a degree of satisfaction in knowing that change is happening. They can be creative and look for new opportunities—new knowledge, a new skill, a new job. How many times have you heard someone say, "I wouldn't have initiated it myself, but that change was the best thing that ever happened to me"?

Why not go out on a limb? That is where the fruit is.

—Will Rogers

When you feel yourself settling into a comfortable routine, ask yourself, Am I getting complacent? Do I accept imperfection too easily? When you feel yourself getting too comfortable, seek discomfort. Rather than sitting securely in the middle of your big flying carpet, stand up and walk to the edge. Look around; look down. Is the ground coming up to meet you? Are you about to crash into a mountain? Good time to change course, right? Yeah, it's scary out on the edge, but now aren't you glad you went there and looked?

Change, challenge, striving, growth—these are all uncomfortable. They require us to leave behind the comfort of relaxing and enjoying any success we may have achieved. There's a lot to be said for comfort, but if you stay comfortable for too long, you begin to take it for granted and you discover it is slipping away. Comfort is a place you catch up to, but it keeps on moving, and catching up to it again is an uncomfortable process.

Second, study those who can beat you. When your team is winning, don't just look smugly at those you're beating; keep your eye on the teams that have a better game. Learn from them. What are they doing that makes them bigger, faster, better, smarter than you? Winners are never satisfied, never complacent.

Third, set your sights high. Challenge yourself. Here's the acid test: if you can achieve your goals doing business as usual, your goals are not high enough. To raise your performance to the next level, set goals that make you worry and sweat—in other words, goals that make you uncomfortable. Your goals should force changes, require tough decisions, and inspire bold actions.

SHELL GAME

To grow, we have to step out of our comfort zone. In that respect, we're a lot like the lobster.

A lobster is a hardy creature, skulking along the sea floor in its tough, durable shell, defending itself with built-in pliers where its hands ought to be (the Edward Scissorhands of the sea). Every so often, however, the lobster undergoes a transformation that interrupts its watery wanderings. It sheds its shell.

There's a downside and an upside to this process. The downside is that once the shell is off, the lobster is soft and squishy, open to the elements, vulnerable to being attacked and eaten by creatures it wouldn't normally have to worry about. It's a very uncomfortable place to be.

The upside is that the lobster can now grow bigger and stronger. Trying to get larger inside a hardened exoskeleton is an exercise in futility, unless the exoskeleton has an emergency exit built in. Once the lobster has departed its old home and formed a new shell, it is a larger, stronger, faster, and more formidable lobster than ever. If something goes wrong with this process and the shell cannot be split open and discarded, the lobster stays small and puny and may not survive long enough to accomplish its main goal in life, which is simply to reproduce.

Like the lobster, we have to crack open our shell and step out from time to time in order to become stronger, swifter, and wiser. Is this process easy? Often it is not. It means letting down our defenses, allowing ourselves to be weak and vulnerable for a time. Our world seems different, more dangerous. We feel naked and insecure.

Even if we don't open ourselves to growth and improvement, if we don't question our boundaries, we cannot ensure that change will not happen. Change will come; it is inevitable. We waste energy when we resist change, and in the end we waste the opportunity to control what happens. Will this change be on our terms? Will we be ready for it? Will the inevitable change mean growth and improvement, or only discomfort and danger?

Our resistance to change is rooted in our fear of the unknown, but we sometimes forget that the unknown often brings good fortune. Think of the good things that have happened to you in your life. How many were unforeseen? Sure, you planned for and achieved some of your successes, but if you look honestly at your life, you will see that much of what has come to you happened without any foresight on your part: the charming small town you chanced across while driving without a map or a plan; the book you found at the garage sale that introduced you to your favorite author; that special person you met at a party you almost didn't attend.

Good things can happen when you break out of last year's shell and take a chance. The more good things you discover by opening yourself to change, the more secure you will feel. The more you understand change and your ability to handle it, the more you begin to see the growth and benefits it can bring. You may learn to enjoy leaving old shells behind!

We cannot become what we need to be by remaining what we are.

—Max DePree

EXPLORE THE EDGE: WINNING TIPS

- Complaceny is the root of mediocrity. Don't get lulled to sleep by your own success. Find those who are the best in your field; watch them, and learn. If you run a retail customer service department, don't just look for the best retailer—look for whoever delivers the best customer service in *any* industry.
- Before you explore the edge, ask yourself the four comforting questions:

  1. Who else has done it?
  2. Can I dip my toe in first?
  3. How bad can it be?
  4. How great can it be?

- Ask yourself, Have I felt uncomfortable lately?
  - If your answer is no, find a way to challenge yourself (for example, set a higher goal, learn a new skill, try a different strategy).
  - Remember, learning and growth occur when you are uncomfortable.

QUIT ANALYZING . . . AND FOLLOW YOUR INTUITION

Intuition becomes increasingly valuable in the new information
society precisely because there is so much data.

—John Naisbitt

ucas considered himself a highly rational thinker and team leader. As head of product development in his company, he liked to analyze each situation, consider the pros and cons, and project the outcomes of the various courses of action available to him. He had made good decisions that had helped build his company up from a small firm with eight people to a major industry player employing hundreds. And he had done it, he thought with pride, by making decisions rationally, not emotionally. Being analytical, he felt, had saved him from making big mistakes.

Lately, however, his company had stagnated. Growth had leveled off and competitors had begun to chip away at its markets. During the last quarter, sales of one of their key products had begun to slip under the onslaught of a more advanced product introduced by a fierce competitor, using a technology his company had been studying but was not yet ready to bring to market. Lucas's engineers had assured him they were ready to gear up for production, but he had held back,

concerned about a few unresolved technical issues and unwilling to bring out a product that might damage his company's reputation.

Lucas knew they had missed the boat and that his engineers were probably correct in saying the technology was proven. Had he been too cautious?

It had not always been so. Lucas's company had been a pioneer in its industry, moving swiftly and surely, beating established companies to market with innovative products that seemed to spring fully formed from Lucas's mind. But as his company grew, Lucas had become hesitant. More was at stake with each decision—more money, more jobs, more people. What if he rushed a decision? The consequences could be disastrous. He added new functions to his department to analyze the potential ramifications of each new development. He held a long series of marathon meetings before making each decision.

Just the other day, though, he had overheard one of his key managers, Kristen, telling someone she wished he would quit overthinking everything and trust his intuition more.

Once he got over the shock of hearing that his leadership was less than perfect, he began to realize that he had, indeed, lost the spontaneity of his early years in business—and the exhilaration that went with it. How was it that most of those early decisions—made on the fly, under pressure, with little or no time to think about the consequences—had turned out to be such good decisions?

He had always looked down on people who claimed to be intuitive. To Lucas, intuition sounded suspiciously like telepathy or clairvoyance, which were, of course, nonsense. But was it possible that the younger Lucas—the one to whom the answers occurred out of nowhere, the one who could make a great decision without thinking twice about it, the one who had created innovative products on a hunch and a hope—had been running on intuition?

ANALYSIS PARALYSIS

One of the most important attributes you possess is the ability to make decisions and move forward. Thinking before taking action is, of course, the right thing to do. However, thinking without acting leads nowhere. Many get stuck in an endless thinking loop and cannot transition to action: "Ready, aim . . . aim . . . aim . . ."

Thomas J. Watson, Sr., who founded IBM in 1924, crafted his company's famous (and ubiquitous) motto from a single word: THINK. The motto epitomized Watson's devout rationalism. "All the problems of the world," he told his employees, "could be solved easily if men were only willing to think."

Watson was a man of action—a world-class salesman—and it probably didn't occur to him that thinkers sometimes fail to recognize that there is a time to quit thinking and take action. Since Watson's time, the global economy has undergone a fundamental shift from hard industry to intellectual capital; employees who can make decisions quickly and instinctively, based on incomplete information, are in demand. IBM realized that the old motto was more than slightly out of sync with the swiftness of modern business practices and later changed the official slogan to make action explicit: THINK. THEN DO.

What the modern IBM knows, along with most social scientists nowadays, is that thinking is only the starting point in the decision-making process. First you think, which involves absorbing all the information you can get your hands on and making as many conscious connections as you can; often this leads to a set of possible decisions. Next, you let your intuition have a go at it, which means *not* thinking about it but just letting your mind drift or working on other things until the answer becomes clear to you. This could happen the moment you wake up in the morning or simply out of the blue when you're thinking about something else entirely. Then, you act.

THAT CERTAIN FEELING

When people use the term "sixth sense," they are often alluding to the power of intuition to foretell events. We've all heard about the friend who took an alternate route to work one day on a hunch, and thereby missed being involved in a terrible pileup on the Interstate; the woman who woke up in the middle of the night thinking about her beloved uncle, unaware that he had died earlier that evening; the fireman who suddenly, without thinking, turned and dashed out of the burning building five seconds before it collapsed.

It's true that we can often sense or get a premonition about something that later happens, but there's nothing magical about it. Out of sight of our consciousness, our subconscious mind puts together everything it knows—a hodgepodge of related and unrelated facts, a patchwork of emotional responses, a vast library of sensory and cognitive experiences, and its uncanny ability to find patterns in chaos—to conjure up a startlingly vivid vision of a thing that's going to happen.

The subconscious, although not formally logical the way we like to think our conscious thought processes are, has the ability to find the hidden relationships between things we know and things that we've forgotten we know. Our friend's subconscious knows that truck traffic on the Interstate is usually heaviest on Friday and that the morning drizzle is likely to make the roads slick, so it whispers to him, Take the surface streets to work. The woman's subconscious is vividly aware of the deteriorating condition of her uncle, whom she saw last Saturday, and projects that he's likely to pass away within a few days, an awareness the woman is emotionally repressing. The fireman's training and experience kick in before he is even aware that he hears the burning roof beams splintering, saving him the bother of asking himself, Is this a good time to get the heck out of here?

Good instincts usually tell you what to do long before your head has figured it out.

—Michael Burke

Intuition works best, naturally, in areas where we have experience and expertise concerning the situation or the people involved. We all have a vast reserve of it, but some hear its inner voice better than others. If we pay attention to it and learn to apply it, intuition can help us perform at our highest potential. Often, however, these signals are weak, and they get covered up by the noise of ordinary life and day-to-day business.

Think of intuition as a shortcut to higher productivity, better insight, more knowledge, innovation, and easier decision making. Intuition is the ability to make quick and sound decisions based on a minimum of information.

Take a look at this next paragraph.

> Cna yuo raed tihs? I cdn'uolt blveiee taht I cluod aulaclty uesdnatnrd waht I was rdanieg. The phaonemnel pweor of the hmuan mnid, aoccdrnig to a rsereeachr at Cmabrigde Uinervtisy, it dseno't mtaetr in waht oerdr the ltteres in a wrod are, the olny iproamtnt tihng is taht the frsit and lsat ltteers be in the rghit pclae. The rset can be a taotl mses and you can sitll raed it whotuit a pboerlm. Tihs is bcuseae the huamn mnid deos not raed ervey lteter by istlef, but the wrod as a wlohe. Azanmig, huh? Yaeh, and I awlyas tghuhot slpeling was ipmorantt!

Now read the following text message (an artifact of our newest language, cellphone-speak) and see if you understand it.

> Im nu N town, cn U drct me 2 yr hse

Isn't it astounding how easily we can decipher words with information that is ambiguous, garbled, or less than complete? We are wired to see underlying patterns, fill in the gaps, straighten out the miscues, and discover the hidden meanings. The same is true of our innate ability to make decisions. It's usually easier, too, if you don't think too hard about it but just let your subconscious do the work—just as it's easier to walk if you don't think about lifting and moving each leg: left, right, left, left—no, right. . . .

For many winners, a defining moment is the first time they use their intuition to "fill in the blanks" and make an important decision in real time, just as we filled in the blanks to read the cellphone text message above.

To make good decisions quickly and intuitively, you need to

- avoid obsessing over details,
- be in tune with your surroundings, and
- keep a clear focus on your objective.

By making these three preconditions part of your everyday actions and habits, you set the stage for your intuition to fire up and start doing its work.

USING YOUR GIFT

Tom Peters called intuition our greatest gift. Many impressive fortunes have been made, thanks to intuition—that hunch, the inner voice, the gut feeling that paved the way to the right decision.

Intuition is a mental tool that's not unique to the gifted and talented; it's a power we all have. It's the feeling we get when what we are seeing doesn't match up with the facts we think we know; it's the sudden move we make without thinking that saves us from disaster; it's the voice that tells us the truth rather than what we would like to hear.

The alternative to the intuition-based approach is rational decision making, which relies mostly on logic and quantitative analysis. You consciously analyze all the options, judge the expected outcomes, and choose the option that is likely to produce the best result.

Rational analysis still plays a crucial role in many situations, especially when you have clear criteria and have to deal with extensive quantitative data, like financial or scientific analysis. In other activities, however, situations arise when rational processes by themselves are not adequate to formulate a decision that you can feel comfortable with. Your intuition can play a valuable role when

- expedient decision making and rapid response are required, e.g., the circumstances leave you no time to go through complete rational analysis;

- the data on which you base your analysis change rapidly;

- the problem is poorly structured;

- the facts and rules that you need to take into account are hard to articulate in an unambiguous way;

- you have to deal with ambiguous, incomplete, or conflicting information; or

- there is no precedent for the circumstances or for the decision that must be made.

80/20 INTUITION

So, how does intuition figure into responsible decision making? Three key attributes characterize the intuitive mode of thinking:

- The process is dominated by your subconscious mind, even if you use your conscious mind to formulate or rationalize the final decision.

- The information is processed in parallel rather than sequentially. Instead of going through a logical sequence of thoughts one by one, you see the situation more as a whole, with different fragments emerging simultaneously.

- You are more connected with your emotions. For example, it may occur to you that an option you consider does not feel right, even though there is no clear logic to prove it.

Applying the 80/20 Principle to our thinking can help us make smarter, faster, more intuitive decisions. The 80/20 Principle (also known as the Pareto Principle) is pervasive in our world:

- 80% of traffic jams occur on 20% of roads.

- 80% of beer is consumed by 20% of drinkers.

- 80% of classroom participation comes from 20% of students.

The 80/20 Principle is also alive and well in most businesses:

- 80% of profits come from 20% of customers.

- 80% of problems are caused by 20% of employees.

- 80% of sales are generated by 20% of sales people.

How does the Pareto Principle apply to decision making? In most situations, you can gather 80 percent of the relevant information in the first 20 percent of the time available. Generally, the remaining 20 percent of the data (which would take the remaining 80 percent of your time to obtain) would not substantially improve the quality of your decision. Your intuition is good enough to organize the data and fill in the gaps, just as it did in those nonsense paragraphs a few pages back.

Specifically, here's how you might apply the 80/20 Principle to your next big decision. First, identify the top five pieces of information you need to make the decision. Then, decide which four of these five are highest in priority. Once you've gathered this information, you will have roughly 80 percent of the information you need, and the remaining 20 percent is less important. Now, harness all of your experience and your intuition to fill in the blanks and make a great decision—even faster!

Trust your hunches. They're usually based on facts filed away just below the conscious level.

—Dr. Joyce Brothers

Many leaders have built winning businesses by following their intuition. Masaru Ibuka, cofounder of Sony Corporation, would drink herbal tea before every business transaction. If he developed a case of indigestion, the deal would be called off. Quipped Ibuka, "I trust my gut more than my mind." It probably won't be as dramatic as it was for Ibuka, but your own intuition can help you make real-time decisions—smart *and* fast.

In 1977, University of Vermont students Lisa Lindahl and her friend Hinda Miller were discussing underwear. Both were avid runners (Lisa ran 30 miles a week), and they were voicing a common complaint among women about the uncomfortable effect of Newton's first law of motion (a body in motion tends to remain in motion) upon the female physique. As a joke, a male friend pulled a jockstrap from the laundry, held it up to his chest, and said, "Look—a jock bra!"

The idea hit Lisa and Hinda simultaneously. The next day, they bought two jockstraps at the campus bookstore, brought them home, and sewed them together. Ta-da! The first sports bra.

The materials and information yet to be connected, the unrecognized potential for a solution, the whimsical spark, and the suddenness of the inspiration are classic signs of intuition at work. In this case, intuition led to a new product that the two women, with the help of fashion designer Polly Smith, turned into a thriving sportswear company, Jogbra. To date, worldwide sales of all sports bras have exceeded half a billion dollars.

Here's the message: Quit analyzing everything. Be ready when intuition strikes. Listen to it. Then, act.

Trust yourself. You know more than you think you do.

—Dr. Benjamin Spock

ALWAYS

FOLLOW YOUR INTUITION: WINNING TIPS

- Make good decisions quickly and intuitively, by

  o avoiding obsessing over details,

  o being in tune with your surroundings, and

  o keeping a clear focus on your objective.

- Apply the 80/20 Principle to your decision making. Think of a decision you're facing. Write down the five most important pieces of information needed to make this decision:

  _____

  _____

  _____

  _____

  _____

  Now, select the four pieces of information above that are the most important. These represent about 80 percent of the information you need. Collect this information as quickly as you can, review it, then harness your experience and intuition to make the decision.

- Write down a problem or goal before you go to bed and meditate on it while falling asleep. Your subconscious mind will make connections and conclusions while you sleep, and your new insights might suprise you when you wake.

QUIT MANAGING YOUR TIME . . . AND MANAGE YOUR ATTENTION

Only one thing has to change for us to know happiness in our lives: where we focus our attention.

—Greg Anderson

Charlie Jones is a sportscaster who has covered several Olympic games in his long career. At the 1996 games in Atlanta, he was assigned to announce the rowing, canoeing and kayaking events—a situation that left him less than thrilled, since it was broadcast at 7 A.M. and the venue was an hour's drive from Atlanta.

What Jones discovered, however, was that it ended up being one the most memorable sports events in his career because he gained a chance to understand the mental workings of these Olympic athletes. Preparing for the broadcast, Jones interviewed the rowers and asked them what they would do in case of rain, strong winds, or breaking an oar. The response was always the same: "That's outside my boat."

After hearing the same answer again and again, Jones realized that these Olympic athletes had a remarkable focus. In their attempt to win an Olympic medal, he wrote, "They were interested only in what they could control—and that was what was going on inside their boat."

ALWAYS

Everything else was beyond their control and not worth expending the mental energy and attention that would distract them from their ultimate goal. Jones says that this insight made the event "by far the best Olympics of my life."

We all have moments when we need to redirect our efforts—or those of others—"inside the boat" to keep ourselves and our team focused. (We may even have to jump out of the boat a few times to rescue those who have gone overboard and drifted away.) We stay inside our boat by managing our attention instead of trying to manage time.

ATTENTION!

You may have been told, perhaps after turning in that term paper three days late, that you had to learn to manage your time. But how do you manage time? Your parents and teachers never explained that, and for a good reason: time is not manageable.

No matter what you do, time marches on at its own pace—tick, tick, tick—and there's nothing you can do to change that (unless you can go pretty close to the speed of light). Time is a great equalizer; it runs at the same speed for everybody, rich or poor, jet pilot or snail farmer. True, time seems to run faster when you're out with friends, slower when you're sitting in the doctor's waiting room, but it's actually chugging along constantly at its normal pace, exactly 168 hours a week, leaving behind a trail of unrecoverable seconds and minutes and hours.

The myth of time management never dies. Many people enroll in "time management" classes and learn techniques like making to-do lists. That's fine. Lists can be useful, even satisfying. It's great to experience that rush—Ahhhh!—as we check something off the list. However, by the end of the day, or the week, or the month, most people discover projects that are still not checked off and some projects they haven't even started. That's when frustration begins to set in. The time is gone, and there's no way to get it back.

You can't manufacture time, you can't reproduce time, you can't slow time down or turn it around and make it run in the other direction.

You can't trade bad hours for good ones, either. About all the time management you can do is to cram as much productive work as possible into each day.

What you *can* manage, however, is your attention.

Attention is a resource we all possess. It's a lot like time. In fact, as long as we are awake, we produce a continuous stream of it. But how effectively do we use this valuable resource? That depends on where we direct our attention and how intensely we keep it focused to produce the desired results.

Your attention reflects your conscious decisions about which activities will occupy your time. The world we live in today is wired, and we are connected as never before, both at work and at home. We are LinkedIn, Facebooked, beeped, Twittered, mapped, GPSed, Web Paged, My Spaced, emailed, blogged, Blackberried, iPhoned, IMed, LexisNexised, Yahooed and Googled with real-time news alerts, stock updates, and traffic reports. Earth-orbiting satellites know where we are every second, how many inches we are from our favorite restaurant, and whether our air bags have deployed. Most of us are so connected that we forget what it's like to be alone with our own thoughts.

Genius is nothing but continued attention.
—Claude-Adrien Helvétius

Most jobs today have multiple responsibilities that are constantly pulling our attention in many directions. If it's true that we can recognize when things need to be done and direct our attention to doing them, then why do we so often run out of time before getting the important things done? It's because we let our attention get diverted. There's usually a plausible reason—an unexpected event or other distraction that seemed important at the time—and we may be able to justify why we were not able to mark the task "done" on our checklist. Or maybe we say we just weren't firing on all eight cylinders that day.

The problem is not time, and it's not our to-do list. We knew how much time we had and we made out a list of what we wanted to do

with it. The problem is that our attention was reallocated to something that was not leading us toward our goals.

So, you can't manage your time. Well, then, how do you manage your attention? Here's what winners do: they identify their priorities, and they know when to say no.

The Yellow Car Phenomenon

One way to manage attention is to harness the power of the Yellow Car Phenomenon. This is a phenomenon that you have undoubtedly experienced and perhaps have wondered about. It happens when something unusual catches your attention—let's say, you see a bright yellow car driving by. You think to yourself, hmm, I don't see one of those very often.

Later that same day, you see two more bright yellow cars. The next day, you see three more. Has there been a sudden invasion of bright yellow cars? No, they've been there all along. The difference is, you've suddenly become aware of them; you have a heightened awareness of yellow cars. We call this the Yellow Car Phenomenon.

First-time expecting parents frequently experience this phenomenon. They have breezed by hundreds of expectant mothers before, never paying much attention. Now that they're pregnant, doesn't it seem like everybody else is too? Amazing, isn't it?

It's the power of personal attention. If your mind is ready to pay attention to something—new people you want to meet, selling opportunities, new applications for an old product, ways to save money, chances to learn a new skill—we tend to draw those things into our consciousness. They have always been there, but now we're paying attention to them.

Instead of paying attention to every single piece of information in our stimulus-rich world, if we really look for those things we want in our life, that's exactly what we will find. Need proof? Just count how many yellow cars you notice today. Now—how many did you see yesterday?

STRIVE TO PRIORITIZE

The first step in managing your attention is to *precisely understand your priorities*. There's a big difference between managing your attention to accomplish priorities and checking off items on your to-do list. Our natural tendency is to do what is fun, convenient, or absolutely necessary at any given time—but your true priorities may not fit into any of those categories. In the absence of clearly defined priorities, you'll find yourself involved in trivial pursuits. These will keep you from doing what needs to be done, but you'll convince yourself that you're accomplishing something.

It's a bad idea to lie to yourself about how productively you're managing your attention. Here's a question to ask yourself that will help you stay on track: If I could accomplish only one thing right now, what would that one thing be? Your answer will quickly identify what your priority should be and where you should be directing your attention. Write the priority at the top of your to-do list and drop secondary priorities to the bottom, or completely off the list.

Time flies. It is up to you to be the navigator.
—Robert Orben

What are your priorities? Stated in simple terms, they are the goals that define your life: being promoted to a higher position, providing a good education for your children, living in a particular community, mastering a new skill. You set the priority and you manage your attention toward that priority.

Dwight D. Eisenhower, the World War II general who went on to become a popular president of the United States, used what is now called the Eisenhower Method for setting priorities. After identifying the tasks confronting him, he drew a square and divided it into four quadrants. One axis was a scale of important to unimportant; the other was urgent to not urgent. Tasks that fell into the unimportant/ not urgent quadrant were dropped. Tasks in the important/urgent sector were accomplished immediately, and by Ike personally. Tasks in the unimportant/urgent quadrant were delegated, and those in the important/not urgent quadrant were assigned due dates and done later personally.

When using the Eisenhower Method, be sure to distinguish between "urgent" and "important" activities. Something that's important is something that is beneficial and should be accomplished—if not right away, then eventually. Something that's urgent is time sensitive, but not necessarily crucial.

As you identify priorities, be realistic about what you *can* accomplish and honest with yourself about what you truly *want* to achieve in your life and work. Where do you want to invest your attention? Although important tasks are your top priorities, most of the time these are not the things that appear to be urgent. Don't be fooled into thinking that whatever seems urgent is worth taking your mind off your most important goal. Eisenhower's mantra was "What's important is seldom urgent, and what's urgent is seldom important."

The Eisenhower Method

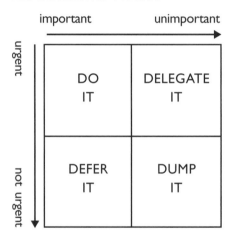

KNOW WHEN TO SAY NO

The sun pours out 600 billion billion kilowatts of energy, yet we can deflect most of its harmful effects with an ultra-thin application of sunscreen or a visor. On the other hand, a laser beam focusing only a few kilowatts of energy can cut a diamond in half or even eradicate certain types of cancer.

Laser-like clarity puts you in the winner's circle. The most important decision to make is to decide what is most important. Your time and energy are precious resources; once you spend them, you don't get them back. Therefore, saying yes to one thing always means saying no to something else. Winners create laser-like clarity by saying no to low-priority activities so they can say yes to the things they are really committed to—their top priorities.

Don't think that saying no just means saying it to others. Most of the time winners say it to themselves—they sacrifice today (by saying no to something that might be fun or tempting) to gain tomorrow's rewards (saying yes to their ultimate goal).

Knowing when to say no is not a once-in-a-while thing; it's a daily winning habit. For example, if you spend two hours in a meeting that doesn't help your team achieve its goals, you pay an opportunity cost by spending time on tasks that do not support your commitments. If you find yourself saying, "That was a waste of time," "Boy, that didn't add any value," or "Why was I attending that meeting?"—these questions may be signs you need to say no. The biggest winners consistently ask themselves, "Is this the best investment of my attention at this moment?" If it is, they get busy. If it's not, they refocus their attention.

If you try to be everything to everyone, you will be nothing to anyone.
—Unknown

When planning your goals, in addition to the things you need to do to achieve the goals, create a "stop doing" list. Write down all activities, tasks, reports, meetings, and projects that do not directly support your goals. This will help you focus your attention more effectively on the things that are most important to you and your team—whether it's at work, at home, or in the community.

So why do we find ourselves saying yes when we should be saying no? Because we've been taken in by several social myths.

Myth 1: If you say no, you'll hurt people's feelings.

Reality: You have no control over another person's feelings. If you're honest in telling the person what your priorities are and why you have to say no, most of the time she will respect that. She would rather hear "Sorry, I can't do it" up front rather than "I'm sorry, I didn't get to it" later. Just tell the truth.

Myth 2: I cannot say no to my subordinates or my boss.

Reality: Actually, you can. You are ultimately responsible for achieving results, and if it's clear that the activity your subordinates or supervisors are suggesting will keep you from accomplishing your priorities, you need to say no and be clear on why you are saying no. If you explain your priorities and they're not in line with the priorities of your subordinates or your boss, something is out of sync.

Myth 3: If I say no to this person, I could irreparably damage the relationship.

Reality: If saying no could damage the relationship, your relationship is probably pretty toxic already. Relationships are damaged more by misunderstandings and unspoken perceptions than by disagreements. If you are open and honest, chances are you'll be able to work through an issue of disagreement.

There is great power in understanding your priorities and maintaining a laser focus. Effectively managing your attention boils down to self-discipline (which, according to former coach Bum Phillips, is "the only discipline that lasts"). There is no set formula. What works for someone else may not work for you because your priorities are different. However, if you know your priorities, focus your attention, and consistently make the best use of your time, you will discover that the right things will get done.

Stay focused. Discover what is important . . . then stick to it.

—Anonymous

MANAGE YOUR ATTENTION: WINNING TIPS

- Pay attention to your "Yellow Cars." Focus your mind on the things you want more of in your life, and you'll find them more often within your reach.

- Learn to focus your attention purposefully.

   o Write down five current challenges you have on your plate.

   _____

   _____

   _____

   _____

   _____

   o Apply the Eisenhower method to the challenges you've listed. Next to each, write "do," "delegate," "defer," or "dump."

- Create a "stop doing" list. Identify three tasks you could quit doing so that you could focus more attention on your top priorities.

   _____

   _____

   _____

QUIT SHOWING INTEREST . . .
AND COMMIT

The quality of a person's life is in direct proportion to his commitment to excellence, regardless of his chosen field of endeavor.
—Vince Lombardi

Most people enjoy turning the calendar to begin a new year. It's a chance to start fresh, with a renewed purpose, and make New Year's resolutions that will ensure the best year ever. In January, resolutions are plentiful: lose weight, read more, maintain a better attitude—you name it, and people are making resolutions to improve something in their life. Hope rises and warms everyone's heart. Surely perfection is finally within reach.

Not.

Somehow most of these ambitions fade to invisibility in the harsh winter light. People genuinely want to improve, but few are prepared to pay the price. The reason is simple: a resolution without an action—a written promise, a passionate commitment—is a waste of time.

Between interest and commitment there is a yawning chasm. Until action happens, there can be no follow-through. There's always a first step, and it's always the hardest one.

Everybody resolves to get into shape. In January, workout facilities are so crowded you have to stand in line for a machine; come April, you can bring your dogsled team and train them on the empty treadmills. The people you saw in January were mostly people who were interested. A few months later, only the committed remain.

What lies between mere interest and the passionate commitment needed to be a winner? There are actions you can take—simple moves and routines that can make the difference. For instance, you can overcome one common barrier between interest and commitment: worry.

DON'T WORRY ABOUT IT

"Lauren," Hank scolded, "you really have got to stop worrying so much. You've made it a full-time job! You worried about James failing high school. You worried that the girls would marry deadbeat husbands who wouldn't provide for them. You worried about our flights getting cancelled before our vacation. Last month, when you had that cold, you even worried about getting the whooping cough, of all things. You worried about all these things, and none of them happened!"

"See!" Lauren exclaimed. "It worked!"

How many of us are like Lauren? Sure, she was making a joke, she knew worrying didn't do any good, but in some situations it seemed to be all she could do. She had long ago fallen into the habit of worrying, and she didn't know how to fall out of it.

When I look back on all these worries, I remember the story of the old man who said on his deathbed that he had had a lot of trouble in his life, most of which never happened.

—Winston Churchill

Research studies have revealed that we typically worry five times as much about things that will never happen as about things that actually do occur. That's a lot of wasted worry! If you're this distracted, you cannot effectively live to up your potential. Worry will drain your energy and stifle your commitment. Every minute you spend worrying is a minute that you're not committing.

One good way to combat worry is to commit to memory Reinhold Niebuhr's "Serenity Prayer": "God grant me the serenity to accept the things I cannot change, the courage to change the things I can, and the wisdom to know the difference."

Once you've accepted the things you cannot change, how do you change the things you can? Simply take a rational approach. Let's say you have a new job and are worried about making a mistake. The worrying mind quickly jumps to a worst-case—and highly unlikely—scenario: If you make a mistake, you'll get fired.

Rationally, you know this is improbable, but how do you prove it to yourself? It's simple. First, you break down the chain of events that would lead to your firing. Then you assign a probability to each event; a rough estimate will do.

Your Worry	Your Estimate of the Chances
I will make a mistake at work.	25%
It will cause a problem.	10%
It will be too late to correct it.	70%
If it causes a problem, my boss will be upset	10%
If he is upset, he will fire me.	5%

So what are the real odds of your being fired? Even though each individual probability is just a rough estimate, the total probability, which is the product of all these individual probabilities, is a good ballpark estimate:

Probability of being fired because of a mistake
$$= 0.25 \times 0.1 \times 0.7 \times 0.1 \times 0.05$$
$$= .0000875, \text{ or } .00875\% \text{ (less than one chance in ten thousand)}$$

Now, doesn't that put things in perspective? This kind of rational approach can help you get a handle on your worries. If the chances of your being fired because of a mistake are less than one in ten thousand, there's really no reason to worry about it.

Now that you've looked the facts in the face, it's time to combat any remaining worries with action.

TAKE POSITIVE ACTION

Life rewards those who seize the moment and take positive action. Action converts interest into commitment. The antidote to worry is purposeful action.

Andrew Carnegie said, "The average person puts only 25 percent of his energy and ability into his work. The world takes off its hat to those who put in more than 50 percent of their capacity and stands on its head for those few and far between souls who devote 100 percent." This is especially true in our degree of commitment. When we fail to invest 100 percent in our goals, we compete against our own potential.

People naturally gravitate to those who are committed to achieving a goal. Total commitment manifests itself as bold action; in a leader this is recognized as genius and power.

Lee: I personally experienced the power of 100 percent commitment (and lack thereof!) when I wrestled with publishing a book for two years. I was consulting and writing leadership articles, and I thought it might be a good time to write a book. I went through all the motions, from working with agents to sending proposals to writers' conferences, but I never seemed to turn the corner from aspiring writer to published author. There was always an obstacle, although I now realize the only obstacle was my tepid commitment to my goal.

The months went by . . . two years and counting. I was interested, but not committed. Then one day at a client's office I saw a big box filled with practical handbooks sitting on his desk. I quickly flipped through one of them and almost shouted, "I can do this!" I jotted down the publisher's name. My moment of commitment had arrived.

With commitment came action, and with the incredibly gracious support of the publisher and coauthor of this book, I had my first book in print six months later. My commitment helped me envision possibilities that I could see only through fully committed eyes.

Committed leaders inspire committed teams. During the most finan-cially challenging time in history for the airline industry, Southwest Airlines' employees voluntarily forfeited $5 million in vacation time and $1 million in pay to help the company stay afloat. Employees also took over the lawn and facility maintenance at corporate headquarters. These employees were simply reflecting the deep commitment—per-sonal and professional—that they felt from their leadership. When you lead with 100 percent commitment, this is the kind of winning spirit you can inspire.

CHOOSE YOUR WORDS

There is power in the words we use, the things we say, and the things we do. Most people greet each other with words that have no power or energy. Think of the last time you heard yourself or someone else respond to a greeting of "How are you?" with "Oh, I'm doing so-so," "Hanging in there," "I'm surviving," or "Not too bad." It probably wasn't much past yesterday.

Now, try this experiment. The next time someone asks, "How are you?", whether it's someone at work or a cashier at the store, respond with strength. Give her an energetic, enthusiastic "Great!" or "Terrific!" It's hard to say this without a smile on your face, and you're likely to get one back. You'll probably feel a surge of energy. Your words will send a message to your mind that will be consistent with feeling Great! or Terrific! To see the results, you have to do this often and with sincere enthusiasm—not robotically. When you do, your subconscious mind begins to act on what you're saying and to make your reality consistent with your thoughts and words.

Choosing the language of commitment creates accountability for get-ting best from yourself and others. Your challenge is to consciously avoid using words that are strength killers, words that sap energy and commitment from your interactions, and ultimately, your actions. Eliminate these words and phrases from your vocabulary:

- I can't
- If
- Doubt

- Try
- I don't think
- I don't have the time
- Maybe
- I'm afraid of
- I don't believe
- It's impossible

But omitting these negative words is not enough. A sports team needs more than just a good defense to win; it also needs a strong offense, so you must also mobilize your own offensive assault with the words you choose. Build positive mental connections, personal strength, and commitment by using the language of commitment:

- I can
- I will
- Expect the best
- Commit
- I know
- I will make the time
- Positively
- I am confident
- I do believe
- All things are possible

The power of your actions is preceded by the power of your words. Choose to speak the language of commitment and watch your winning words turn into winning ways!

Do, or do not. There is no try.

—Yoda

WRITE IT DOWN

Most people who set goals for themselves do so only in their heads. This is a mistake. Goals can get swamped by the rush of everyday thoughts and actions, and the exact wording and significance may get lost, if not the entire goal. Without a tangible goal, interest soon fades to inaction and people are once again drifting aimlessly through life.

The first and most important step toward making a goal real is to write it down. Write it exactly as you want to remember it—make it specific and clear—and keep it where you can refer to it. Scribble it in your palm, tack it to the bulletin board, type it into your screen saver, seal it in an envelope and mail it to yourself.

Personal commitment begins with a crystal-clear understanding of what you are trying to accomplish, including all the specifics. You need to *see* the goal, both in your mind and in your own written words. Why? Because the physical act of writing it down helps you be clear on your purpose and is essential to getting it firmly planted in both your conscious and your subconscious. Your commitment on paper plants the seeds of commitment in your mind.

In 1990, while he was still relatively unknown, comedian Jim Carrey wrote a check to himself for $10 million for "acting services rendered." As Carrey later explained, it wasn't about money. He knew that if he was making that much, he'd be working with the best people on the best material. As they say in Hollywood, the rest is history.

Benjamin Franklin made a list of traits he wanted to either get rid of or cultivate. He graded himself on his progress or regression every day—not yearly, weekly, or monthly, but every day. His question to himself was "Did I get closer to accomplishing my goals, or did I lose ground today?" His way of handling the question was typical of his practical mindset; he was committed enough to his goals to take the time to measure his progress. In this way he kept his goals constantly in view, making sure that each day he took at least one step toward achieving them.

Written goals—personally set, continually visualized, and important enough to be worth paying the price for success—have a mysterious way of coming true.

David: When my son, Michael, left home for college, he proudly announced that he had set his academic goal for his first semester. I had taught him to be a goal setter; he knew the importance of mentally creating a goal and then physically doing what was necessary to make the goal happen. When I asked what his goal was, Michael told me, "Don't worry—I've got it under control." He handed me a sealed envelope and told me not to open it until he came home.

I expected that he would adjust to being away from home, get involved in activities and events, have a good time, and stay off academic probation. I didn't know what his expectations were for himself.

At the end of the first semester, Michael came home, and a few days later his transcript arrived from the school. He opened it and showed me his grade point average: 3.8.

Then he asked for the envelope he had left with me. Together we opened it. Inside was a slip of paper with a number written on it: 3.8.

Michael told me that all semester he had focused on getting a 3.8 GPA. He had written it everywhere: in his wallet, on his mirror, on the door, everywhere he looked. Every day he measured his progress toward his goal, striving for the 3.8, even higher if he could. He was so passionate about his goal that he measured every action in terms of whether it would help him accomplish it.

He was more than interested—he was committed.

COMMIT WITH PASSION

Commitment isn't just checking off progress toward the goal; it's an attitude, an approach to life. People who are only interested lose that interest as soon as they leave their comfort zone. Those who are truly committed ignore discomfort and keep moving forward through the most daunting difficulties.

In 1921, in Kane, Pennsylvania, history was made: for the first time, an appendectomy was performed using only local anesthesia.

Dr. Evan O'Neill Kane, chief surgeon at Kane Summit Hospital and son of the town's founder, Thomas L. Kane, had been contending for years that surgery under local anesthesia was far safer than using general anesthesia, the conventional practice. Many of his colleagues were interested in his theory but not committed enough to test it on their patients. They needed proof.

Dr. Kane's patients were not excited about being a part of a laboratory study, either. After several weeks of searching for a volunteer to prove his theory, the surgeon finally found a candidate who was willing to help test the theory while undergoing an appendectomy.

When it was time for the surgery, the patient was prepped and wheeled into the surgical suite. Dr. Kane then took the scalpel and performed the surgery. The procedure went as planned and the patient complained only of minor discomfort. Two days after the procedure, the patient was dismissed from the hospital ward. Thanks to the brave volunteer, Dr. Kane had demonstrated that local anesthesia was not just a viable alternative to general anesthesia, it was preferable.

Who was the courageous volunteer for Dr. Kane's experimental surgery? It was Dr. Kane himself! Using only local anesthesia, he removed his own appendix. He was so committed to his belief that he was willing to become a patient in order to persuade other patients to trust their doctor. Many were interested in knowing if the procedure would work; Dr. Kane alone was committed to finding out.

Between interest and commitment lie as many obstacles as you want to put in your way. If you're committed to overcoming those obstacles, there's always a way over or around them. Remember:

- Worry forestalls commitment.

- Action conquers worry.

- Words affect actions.

- Writing down the goal opens the gate to action.

- Commitment with passion overcomes all obstacles.

How committed are you to your goals? Are you willing to test your commitment under the knife?

COMMIT: WINNING TIPS

- Manage your worry.

  - Restrict your time for worrying about your problems. Even during these limited times of worry, follow up immediately with specific, positive action.

  - Start a "gratitude journal" to help you keep things in perspective and minimize unnecessary worry. Every day, write down something you're thankful for. Make your first journal entry right here! Write down two things you are grateful for today:

  _____

  _____

- Take positive action.

  - Put your goals into words and pictures—then invest your time and energy, every day, to get closer to your goals.

  - Surround yourself with people who are equally committed. Commitment (like apathy) is contagious. Write the names of two people who can help you keep your commitments:

  _____

  _____

- Speak the language of commitment to create accountability for getting the best from yourself and others. Write down two noncommittal words you tend to use. Next to them write words of commitment you can replace them with.

  Noncommittal words   Words of commitment

  _____   _____

  _____   _____

QUIT MOVING . . . AND BE STILL

Learning how to be still, to really be still and let life happen—
that stillness becomes a radiance.

—Morgan Freeman

Lucas was pleased with the way his product development team, with chief engineer Kristen out in front, had taken the reins and begun making more and more of the operational decisions. Instead of holding an endless string of meetings, Lucas had decided to let the team—these talented people he had interviewed, hired, and trained—do the job they were capable of, and to simply monitor and ratify their decisions. It had not been easy to break his old, cautious habit of overanalyzing, but somehow, intuitively, he had concluded that it was the right thing for him to do.

Still, Lucas felt that he was falling behind in his own responsibilities, making strategic decisions about future product development. The adventurous spirit that had guided him earlier in his career, the creativity that had spawned so many of his company's innovative products and put his company far ahead of its competitors, had waned. There were always products waiting to be "discovered," but other explorers now did more of the discovering.

ALWAYS

He applied his reasoning skills to the problem. He accumulated industry production data, kept up with the latest technological developments, and analyzed the marketing trends, but somehow the answers just didn't come.

Lucas felt drained, out of ideas, washed up. Burnt out.

He decided to take a week off and do nothing. Well, not exactly nothing. On Monday he drove down to the lake and spent the afternoon tinkering with his boat and chatting with his fishing buddies. He thoroughly enjoyed his afternoon, although he found himself wishing he had a better tool for changing the spark plugs.

Tuesday afternoon he hung out with his two boys to give his wife some time with her mother. This made the two top women in his life very happy—always a good policy—and gave Lucas an excuse to tell the boys about his glory days as a basketball star. They went to the park, where Lucas demonstrated his jump shot. Both boys then shot a few hoops and, since their scoring percentage turned out to be greater than his and since a few other boys showed up and started a game, Lucas retired to the bench and watched them play.

He noticed a few other parents on nearby benches. One of them was reading "Jack and the Beanstalk" to her small daughter. The name "Jack" reminded Lucas of something one of his shop managers had said when recommending a cousin to him: "He'd be good anywhere on the line. He's a jack of all trades." Lucas made a mental note to talk more with his manager and to follow up with the personnel department.

On the way home, with the boys strapped into the back seat of his large SUV watching the overhead DVD, Lucas thought about how much better it would be to drive a crossover vehicle. It would get better mileage, be more maneuverable and more pleasant to drive, and would hold almost as much as this behemoth he had been driving for six years. Time to buy a smaller, more versatile people hauler, he thought. Something that combined the smooth ride and quick handling of a regular sedan with the cargo capacity of a station wagon.

Wednesday was going to be a day with nothing on his schedule—a rarity for Lucas. It made him restless from the start. He tried to watch the morning television shows but kept wandering off into other rooms. He picked up the book he had left on his nightstand but couldn't get back into it. Finally he decided to go for a drive.

He got into his wife's new sports car and headed for the highway but soon found himself inexplicably in the parking lot of his company. So much for his promise to take a week off.

He sat at his desk doodling on a sheet of paper, his mind restless, trying to look busy to the confused administrative assistant who kept coming into his office, glancing at him, and going out again.

Then, before he even realized it, he saw his breakthrough product. It would be a combination of several current products, using both the old and the new technologies, that would be more versatile, offer more advantages, and appeal to more markets than any of the current products separately. It was so simple he began to worry immediately that a competitor might already have beat him to it. But he didn't think they had, and if he acted quickly, he could control the market.

He flashed back to the early days of his career, when he was spinning out ideas faster than he could write them down, turning out fresh new products that blew the competition away, when every decision was fast and easy and right. This is the way it had felt.

STOP, LOOK, AND LISTEN

The blinding speed of today's information-saturated, time-deprived, hypercompetitive world forces us to run, run, run just to keep pace. Alarm! Snooze button. Alarm! Shower. Shave. Computer on. Phone on. Check headlines. Check voice mail. Check email. Google dog groomer. Make dinner reservations. Microwave breakfast. Drive to office. Check email. Check schedule. Text Junior about afternoon pickup time for soccer practice. Join global teleconference in progress. Answer incoming text message. Log out early to handle phone storm—and that's just the first hour.

Accessibility through technology can be a double-edged sword—a blessing in terms of our productivity and material prosperity, but a curse on our peace of mind and ability to relax and enjoy life. Sometimes we seem to be human doings rather than human beings. We rush around madly in pursuit of our goals, and when problems arise, we are pulled toward them to find the answers—but the more deeply we get involved with the problems, the more elusive the goal becomes.

When you're busy being a human doing, you're usually too focused on the job to stand back and look at the big picture. You're too rationally involved in your goal to give your creativity free rein, to see the natural solutions to problems that stymie you.

Did you ever drive a car at night in a thick fog? If you have, you know that you can see farther down the road if you use your low beams, because your high beams just reflect off the fog and blind you. It's the same thing if you're trying to solve a problem in your life or your business: the high-intensity approach sometimes blinds you by putting your focus on unimportant issues rather than the real problem. But if you use your low beams instead—get away from the problem and let your creative intuition do its work—often the answer emerges and the path to the goal becomes clearer to you.

Creativity is a playful process; it needs recreation. You need to get your mind out of the dark, airless classroom and send it out to the playground where it can run around and have some fun. The way to find the answers is to stop moving for a while and let things settle down. Be still. Relax. Be quiet. Look around. Listen.

Lee: My youngest daughter has a special area in her room where she can chill and relax. She calls it her "chillax zone." Although your chillax zone might not have big pink pillows and a fluffy white carpet, we all need to make a time and place that offers us mental space. Your space might be your car as you drive home after work, a reading or meditation corner in your house, your bathtub, your gym, a nearby park where you walk—anywhere you can be alone with your thoughts. The thinking, planning, and reflection you do in this space helps you get off the treadmill and rise above the hurly-burly of your everyday world to gain a better perspective on yourself, your situation, and your dreams.

ZONE OUT

How, exactly, in today's hyperactive and attention-demanding world, do we switch from high to low beams? We can do it by carving out our own mental space, a place in the mind where we can go for some quiet time, where we can be still and think clearly, free from the barrage of inputs.

You must learn to be still in the midst of activity and to be vibrantly alive at rest.

—Indira Gandhi

To get into your chillax zone, you don't actually have to go on vacation or head for the spa. All you've got to do is change the scenery in your mind. Instead of trudging along the dusty trail following the ruts of the wagon train, fly yourself to the top of the mountain where you can be still, relax, and dream while you gaze out over the world below.

Here are some of the ways you can create some mental space:

- Take a few moments each day to clear your mind of distractions. Visualizing a chalkboard being erased often helps with this exercise.

- Pay attention to energy shifts in your physical body. When do they happen? The timing might tell you what is piquing your interest, causing you to worry, raising your adrenaline level, creating stress, and otherwise keeping you on edge.

- Keep an Intuition Notebook to record all "coincidences"— things you had a gut feeling would happen, but only after the fact realized that your gut was giving you a hint. (It was your intuition! Learn to listen to it.)

- Follow your hunches. Prepare to be amazed where they lead.

- Turn off that car radio. Giving your ears a rest can free your inner voice.

- At home, turn off the computer, the television, and the music. Spend a half hour or so in quiet meditation or contemplation.

ALWAYS

- Notice scents around you. What emotions or memories do they stir up?

- Spend time each week enjoying nature.

When you stop moving, your world gets quieter. You don't hear the babble of people working all around you, the rustle of information, the pinging of emotion, the roar of the wind past your ears. All that noise, gone—and then you can truly listen.

You will find that there are two kinds of listening that come naturally when the noise has subsided.

1. You can listen to yourself, because your heart and your mind will have things to say that can only be whispered.

2. You can listen to others, because they have things to say that you don't ordinarily hear over the rumble of what you think they're saying.

LISTEN TO YOURSELF

Lucas had a problem. He couldn't decide what his team's next step should be. All his experience and knowledge didn't seem to be enough. His mind knew the answer but was unable to tell him because the noise of everyday business drowned out its quiet voice. So when Lucas took a mental break, his subconscious mind began to focus its spotlight on things Lucas should be listening more carefully to.

"Listen," it said, and Lucas saw "Jack and the Beanstalk" on the children's book cover in the park, which made him recall the "jack of all trades" his team member had mentioned. A jack of all trades is a combination of many skills in a single person. "Listen to your mind," it said: the tool Lucas had envisioned while working on his boat was a tool combining several functions, and the new crossover automobile that Lucas suddenly thought about buying combined the best features of several different vehicle types.

So when Lucas drifted back to his office early, his subconscious mind took him there, primed to the bursting point with a new idea ready to see daylight.

To get out of your rut, stop moving. When Lucas stopped moving, his thinking became more receptive to outside influences. The noise receded, and he could hear the quiet voices of other people and his own mind telling him the answer. Always playful and creative, these voices posed the answer in the form of a riddle that he had to ponder, subconsciously, until it all came together in a rush of insight.

Some 20 years ago, Max Perutz, a pioneer of molecular biology, wrote that many people work too much and read and think too little. He also lamented the disappearance of leisure time in academic life. Many ideas, explained Professor Perutz, come to scientists while they are doing something else—usually something simple and repetitive, such as mowing the lawn or driving a car. In 1948 Swiss inventor George de Mestral and his dog went hiking and came home covered with burrs. When he examined a burr under the microscope, de Mestral saw that it was covered with tiny hooks. This gave him the idea for a fastener that he called "velcro," a combination of "velour" and "crochet." His inner voice spoke—and he listened.

If you surrender completely to the moments as they pass, you live more richly in those moments.

—Anne Morrow Lindbergh

Something inside spoke to Alexander Fleming, too. The Scottish scientist was growing cultures of *Staphylococcus* bacteria in his lab in 1928. He went on vacation, and when he returned he found his cultures contaminated with the mold *Penicillium notatum*. He noticed that around each mold organism there was a distinct circle in which no *Staphylococcus* grew. Fleming quickly recognized that the mold was emitting a powerful antibiotic, and from this discovery penicillin, the first wonder drug, was born.

These breakthroughs occurred while their inventors were "being still." It may seem counterintuitive to put aside your work in order to accomplish something great, but great ideas often come when you're relaxed and out of your work routine.

Listening to your inner thoughts is a good way to find out what you're thinking—who you really are, what you truly want, where you're going.

LISTEN TO OTHERS

For some presidents, one of the most tiresome duties is standing in a receiving line to welcome guests to the White House. Franklin D. Roosevelt, who always preferred more substantive work, quickly grew bored when he had to perform this social function. He detested the small talk and suspected that nobody really listened to what anybody else was saying.

On one occasion, to amuse himself, he performed an experiment. As he shook hands, he greeted each visitor with the comment, "I murdered my grandmother this morning."

The guests would respond with polite nonsense of their own: "That's wonderful! You're doing such great work! Keep it up!"

One guest, however, an ambassador from another country whose first language was not English, listened solemnly. He looked into Roosevelt's eyes, clasped his hand tenderly, and replied, "I'm sure she had it coming."

Whether this story is true or not, it should be. The truth is, we often don't listen carefully to what another person is saying. We're too busy thinking about what we're going to say next. The result can be embarrassing:

"Your daughter was in my history class eight years ago. She was one of my best students."

"How nice. What do you do for a living?"

Even if you're hearing most of what is being spoken out loud, you may not be getting the full message. Body language, inflection, expression, tone of voice are important components in what is being communicated. Beyond that, it helps to know things about the person that may remain unspoken: what is her background, her profession, her personal history, her relationships with others, her relationship to the truth? Is what she's saying likely to be highly accurate, or is she delusional?

Winners—whether in business, at home, or in the community—generally spend at least 50 percent of their time listening rather than talking. The more authority and responsibility you have, the more important it is for you to listen. People in positions of respect tend to hear less truth spoken to them than others; nobody wants to tell the boss the bad news. The higher you rank in any organization, the more filtered the information you receive. This is why many bosses have blind spots about their own errors or faults. This is also why a good leader encourages her team to discuss problems openly and frankly with her and tell her if they disagree and why. A good leader listens carefully for the truth, because it can keep her out of trouble.

As frequent advisors to a number of different organizations, the authors are well aware that the primary value a consultant brings to his clients is a fresh perspective. An outside advisor is immune to the organization's "noise" and can more quickly and easily identify problems and solutions. The very nature of being an outside party affords the consultant mental space.

Master the art of being still. Enjoy the quiet—and listen. Listen to yourself; listen to others. The quiet voices that speak to you when you're relaxed, still, and receptive can tell you things you know but don't know you know.

Everything has been said before, but since nobody listens we have to keep going back and beginning all over again.

—André Gide

BE STILL: WINNING TIPS

- Create your own mental space to think, plan, and reflect.

  o Turn off your car radio.

  o Turn off your computer.

  o Go for a walk.

  o Spend some quiet time in nature.

  o Use your "chillax zone" to get off that treadmill.

- Spend more of your conversation time listening than speaking.

  o Listen, really listen, to yourself and others.

  o Focus on all communication cues, not just the words.

- Slow down to speed up.

  o Stop and listen to what others are telling you.

  o Be open to and reflect on input from other sources.

  o Let problems and ideas "marinate" in a resting mind.

QUIT STRIVING FOR SUCCESS . . .
AND SEEK SIGNIFICANCE

Try not to become a man of success, but rather try to become a man of value.

—Albert Einstein

This is a tale of two Eddies.

Al "Scarface" Capone was the king of organized crime in Chicago in the 1920s, and his lieutenant was a lawyer people called "Easy Eddie." Eddie helped Al run his affairs—bootleg liquor, gambling, prostitution, murder—and hide them from the authorities. Eddie was very good at his job, which was basically keeping Scarface out of jail.

Capone paid him well for his services. Eddie had a big house, servants, a fine car. He lived as well as an industrial baron, and he didn't lose sleep over what was going on around him. Life was for the successful.

But Easy Eddie did have one soft spot—his beloved son. Eddie lavished him with clothes, a car, a good education, the best of everything money could buy. But there was one other thing Easy Eddie wanted his son to have, something Easy Eddie himself did not have: a good name.

So one day Easy Eddie made a difficult and dangerous decision. In 1930 he asked a reporter friend to put him in touch with the Internal

Revenue Service. He would reveal how Capone made his money and dodged taxes. He became what a top government investigator later said was "one of the best undercover men I have ever known."

Capone was tried and found guilty of tax evasion and sentenced to 11 years in prison. A few years later, Easy Eddie was shot to death in his car by killers unknown.

The Navy's first Medal of Honor aviator of World War II was another Eddie, a superb fighter pilot whose many friends called him "Butch." In the Southwest Pacific in early 1942, the Japanese launched a bomber attack on his aircraft carrier, the USS *Lexington*. Butch and his wingman were the only flyers aloft close enough to intercept the enemy formation, and the wingman's guns were jammed. Butch dived at the bombers again and again, weaving in and out of the formation with all six 50-caliber guns blazing, shooting down five of the nine enemy planes and so disrupting the attack that none of the bombs fell on target. Butch's bravery and skill were credited with saving the ship, and he became a national hero.

By late 1943, because of the success of the U.S. Navy's flight tactics, the Japanese bombers had changed their operations and were attacking after dark. To counter this new tactic, Butch and his squadron were developing the Navy's first night operations. Airborne radar and navigation equipment were primitive in 1943, nowhere near as capable as the modern gear that makes night operations routine. In this risky environment, the Navy's first Medal of Honor aviator was shot down. Neither he nor his plane was ever found.

In 1945 the U.S. Navy named a new destroyer after him: the USS *O'Hare* (DD-889). The city of Chicago went a step further. To honor their hometown hero, in 1949 its citizens named their new airport after him: O'Hare International.

In the end, "Easy Eddie" O'Hare, Al Capone's top lawyer, had found a way to transform his life from one of success—tainted though it was by the crimes he abetted—to a life of significance. He gave the world a principled son, Edward "Butch" O'Hare, who redeemed the family name.

SUCCESS SAYS WHO?

What is success? Is it money? Fame? A house with a swimming pool with a built-in spa? Achieving an ambitious professional goal? A beautiful spouse and two point three beautiful children?

Most people's definition of success is conceived in terms of something they have acquired. It's all about the first person: I, me, mine. People who are just getting started in their careers are often the ones most influenced by displays of material wealth and personal prestige; they want to be like the people they see who are considered successful.

Only later in life do many people begin to understand that success in terms of one's own achievement and satisfaction is hollow. It has a short shelf life; once the trophy is on the shelf, it loses its sparkle and leaves you hungry for more. But with age sometimes comes wisdom, and wise people know that true success, and life's greatest satisfaction, lies in helping others. That is where significance is found.

The key to realizing a dream is to focus, not on success but significance— and then even the small steps and little victories along your path will take on greater meaning.

—Oprah Winfrey

Throughout history, the people we remember with reverence are those who have done things to benefit others. It's worth noting that some people we now think of as heroes were originally considered scoundrels but later got their reputations rehabilitated by doing something that gave their lives real significance. Steel tycoon Andrew Carnegie was ruthless in pursuit of wealth, feared by many, in the late nineteenth century; today most people associate his name with libraries. Why? Because he poured 90 percent of the fortune he had amassed back into the community, much of it in the form of thousands of public libraries in small towns that had few other cultural resources. The Rockefeller and Ford Foundations are other examples of success transformed into significance.

ALWAYS (handwritten, above "NEVER" which is crossed out)

TIME, TALENT, TREASURE

You don't have to become an industrial baron and make a billion dollars to live a life of significance. All you have to do is share the resources you now have. However insignificant you may think they are, they are of greater value to someone not so fortunate as you.

The straightforward way to live a life of significance is simply to share your three T's: time, talent, and treasure. Our lives are meant to be given away—to significant purposes, to loving families, to friends in need, to lasting relationships. Find a way that your gifts can serve others. Your time, energy, and money are precious resources—they are limited, and you are the sole owner. If you spend them in one area, you can't spend them in another. When we say yes to one thing, by default we are saying no to something else. The key to winning is to say yes to the significant things in your life.

Time. It's a paradox of life that only by giving away our time do we make our lives meaningful, for time is the most precious gift of all. The time we spend playing with a child or grandchild, chatting with a bedridden friend, mowing a neighbor's lawn, teaching another adult to read cannot be measured in money but is priceless. And life rewards those who donate their time, first in terms of their own satisfaction and the good opinion of others, later in ways they can never foresee. The time may come when _you_ need a hand, and there will be many more hands offering help than you can count.

You can have all the success you want by helping enough other people achieve all the success they want.

—Zig Ziglar

Talent. There's something especially rewarding about applying your best talents toward the benefit of others. One outstanding example of this is Médecins Sans Frontières (MSF), also known as Doctors Without Borders. A secular, non-governmental humanitarian organization funded mostly by private donations, MSF was founded in 1971 by a group of French doctors to come to the aid of people in areas of the world where poverty, war, political violence, or natural disaster had left people vulnerable to disease. Its 60,000 doctors, nurses, medical professionals, logistics experts, and water and sanitation engineers work as unpaid or low-paid volunteers, using their training and skills not where they will be materially rewarded but where they can do the greatest good.

The way to make the greatest contribution with your talent is by recognizing and using your strengths. Most types of sports equipment—golf clubs, tennis racquets, baseball bats—have a certain spot called the "sweet spot." Hitting the ball with that spot yields optimal results: a long drive down the fairway, a swift crosscourt return, a home run. If you've experienced it, you know that when you hit the sweet spot you barely feel it, but the ball seems to know where you want it to go.

> *Successful people are always looking for opportunities to help others. Unsuccessful people are always asking, "What's in it for me?"*
> —Brian Tracy

Okay, maybe you're not an athletic superstar. But whatever you endeavor to do, there's a sweet spot that you sometimes hit that makes everything seem easier. Sometimes the sweet spot can be thought of as a set of skills that you can apply to something you want to accomplish, such as helping others. Want to know an easy way to find your sweet spot? Answer the following two questions, and think about how your answers intersect:

1. What am I absolutely passionate about?

2. Which tasks are easy and natural for me?

Did you know the average person possesses between 500 and 700 different skills and abilities? Finding that skill or ability that's right in your sweet spot is a first step toward seeking significance. This ensures the highest and best use of your talents toward your goals and toward helping others. Wouldn't it be great to be living and working in your sweet spot? You'd always be "in the zone."

Most of us recognize the feeling of significance we get when we're living in our sweet spot. Others tell us we make it look easy, that we really excel, that we seem to be having a ball, that we're "in the zone."

When was the last time others said something like this to you? What were you doing? Like finding any sweet spot, it's worth hitting these questions around for awhile and finding your answers. Then you'll be ready to serve up your winning shot.

Treasure. You don't have to be rich to donate your treasure to others—an insignificant part of your modest holdings can be a fortune to others—but stories of truly generous wealthy people lift all our spirits. Here's one.

In 1981, business leader and self-made millionaire Eugene Lang looked out at the faces of the 59 African American and Puerto Rican sixth-graders who had come to hear him speak. Years earlier, Lang had attended this same school in East Harlem. Now, he wondered how he could get these children to listen to him. What could he say to inspire these students when, statistically, most would probably drop out of school before graduation?

Finally, scrapping his notes, he spoke from his heart. "Stay in school," he told them. "If you do, I'll help pay the college tuition for every one of you."

At that moment, he changed the life of every student in the room. For the first time, they had hope—hope of achieving more than their older brothers and sisters, hope of living a better life than their parents and neighbors.

Six years later, nearly 90 percent of that class graduated from high school, and true to his promise, Lang made it possible for them to attend college. A few years later he founded the "I Have a Dream" Foundation, which has supported similar projects in 57 cities, assisted by more than 200 sponsors helping more than 12,000 disadvantaged students with academic support and guidance through high school and a college education.

GIVE TO RECEIVE

There's a Chinese proverb that says, "If you continually give, you will continually have." The person who first said that may have been a farmer, because creating a life of significance is a lot like growing bamboo. One planted, bamboo may take up to two years before sprouting through the surface. It requires the right combination of water, sunlight, care, and feeding to build a strong root structure and foundation for growth, and none of this growing foundation is visible aboveground. But once it sprouts, bamboo can grow 100 feet in two weeks. Patience is a prerequisite for the bamboo farmer—and for anyone who seeks to build a life of significance. Be impatient to plant the seeds of significance, but patient enough to nurture them and watch them grow.

I feel the capacity to care is the thing which gives life its deepest significance.

—Pablo Casals

SEEK SIGNIFICANCE: WINNING TIPS

- Our relationships are a primary source of purpose and significance in our lives. Ask yourself each day:

  o How do I define success?

  o What will I do today to create significance in my life?

- Look for ways to invest your three T's—time, talent, and treasure—in other people.

- Live in your sweet spot by answering these questions:

  o What am I absolutely passionate about?

  o Which tasks am I really good at?

NEVER QUIT QUITTING!

So—quitters always win?

Yes!

All right, maybe quitters don't always win. After all, perseverance is also a key to winning. You've got to keep working until the job is finished.

But the key point is that perseverance counts only if you're doing the right thing. If you're doing the wrong thing, and you keep on doing the wrong thing, you'll never win.

So you do have to quit. In order to do the very best thing, you have to quit doing the next-best thing. You have to swap pretty good habits for really great ones.

Here's how you can win by quitting:

- You can quit going along to get along, take the wheel, and gain control of your own fate.

- You can quit enjoying the comforts of certainty and challenge your mind to discover the edge where the known meets the unknown.

- You can quit overanalyzing every issue and let your intuition apply its vast skills and resources to find the answers.

- You can quit trying to manipulate the flow of time and instead learn to focus your attention on the most productive use of your time.

- You can quit resolving to pursue your most ambitious goals and truly commit to them—in words, on paper, and with passion.

- You can quit rushing around to get things done, sit back and enjoy the quiet, listen to your own mind and the words of others, and discover new insights into your world.

- You can quit focusing entirely on the standard vision of success and achieve significance and satisfaction by giving others the benefit of your time, talents, and treasure.

Quitting wisely means knowing when and what to quit. But this knowledge changes by the day and by the situation—which means you must never quit questioning, never quit examining your approach, your results, and your assumptions. In short, never quit learning.

Your life is your own learning lab, where you can build winning habits. Watch the people around you. You can learn nuggets of excellence from a father-in-law, a minister, a speaker at a professional association, a work colleague, your child's school teacher, a scout troop leader, or a particularly helpful salesperson at a local store. Observe, read, ask, listen, and learn.

There are lessons to be learned in everything your team does. Look for opportunities in post-project reviews, customer meetings, conflicts with others, changes in priorities, miscommunications and mistakes. If you never quit learning, you build your competence—and competence builds confidence. Confidence is key for winners.

Learn when and what to quit—and keep on winning!

You don't have to be great to get started,
but you do have to get started to be great.

Start quitting today
to keep winning tomorrow!

Winning Tips Summary

1. Quit Taking a Ride . . . and Take the Wheel

- Plan for the unexpected.

  - Write down three things that, however unlikely, could adversely affect a current project or goal.

    _____

    _____

    _____

  - For each of the unexpected events you listed, write down some ways you might respond. It's not what happens to you, but how you choose to handle it, that makes you a winner.

    _____

    _____

    _____

- Whenever you see a problem, resist assigning blame; instead:

  - Brainstorm as many potential solutions as you can before you evaluate any of them.

  - Challenge yourself (and others) to find the best solution.

ALWAYS

2. Quit Getting Comfortable . . . and Explore the Edge

- Complacency is the root of mediocrity. Don't get lulled to sleep by your own success. Find those who are the best in your field; watch them, and learn. If you run a retail customer service department, don't just look for the best retailer—look for whoever delivers the best customer service in *any* industry.

- Before you explore the edge, ask yourself the four comforting questions:

  1. Who else has done it?

  2. Can I dip my toe in first?

  3. How bad can it be?

  4. How great can it be?

- Ask yourself, Have I felt uncomfortable lately?

  o If your answer is no, find a way to challenge yourself (for example, set a higher goal, learn a new skill, try a different strategy).

  o Remember, learning and growth occur when you are uncomfortable.

3. QUIT ANALYZING . . . AND FOLLOW YOUR INTUITION

- Make good decisions quickly and intuitively, by

  o avoiding obsessing over details,

  o being in tune with your surroundings, and

  o keeping a clear focus on your objective.

- Apply the 80/20 Principle to your decision making. Think of a decision you're facing. Write down the five most important pieces of information needed to make this decision:

  _____

  _____

  _____

  _____

  _____

  Now, select the four pieces of information above that are the most important. These represent about 80 percent of the information you need. Collect this information as quickly as you can, review it, then harness your experience and intuition to make the decision.

- Write down a problem or goal before you go to bed and meditate on it while falling asleep. Your subconscious mind will make connections and conclusions while you sleep, and your new insights might suprise you when you wake.

ALWAYS
(handwritten, with "NEVER" struck through)

4. QUIT MANAGING YOUR TIME . . . AND MANAGE YOUR ATTENTION

- Pay attention to your "Yellow Cars." Focus your mind on the things you want more of in your life, and you'll find them more often within your reach.

- Learn to focus your attention purposefully.

  o Write down five current challenges you have on your plate.

  _____

  _____

  _____

  _____

  _____

  o Apply the Eisenhower method to the challenges you've listed. Next to each, write "do," "delegate," "defer," or "dump."

- Create a "stop doing" list. Identify three tasks you could quit doing so that you could focus attention on your top priorities.

  _____

  _____

  _____

5. QUIT SHOWING INTEREST . . . AND COMMIT

- Manage your worry.

    o Restrict your time for worrying about your problems. Even during these limited times of worry, follow up immediately with specific, positive action.

    o Start a "gratitude journal" to help you keep things in perspective and minimize unnecessary worry. Every day, write down something you're thankful for. Make your first journal entry right here! Write down two things you are grateful for today:

    _____

    _____

- Take positive action.

    o Put your goals into words and pictures—then invest your time and energy, every day, to get closer to your goals.

    o Surround yourself with people who are equally committed. Commitment (like apathy) is contagious. Write the names of two people who can help you keep your commitments:

    _____

    _____

- Speak the language of commitment to create accountability for getting the best from yourself and others. Write down two noncommittal words you tend to use. Next to them write words of commitment you can replace them with.

    Noncommittal words   Words of commitment

    _____   _____

    _____   _____

ALWAYS (handwritten, with "NEVER" struck through)

6. QUIT MOVING . . . AND BE STILL

- Create your own mental space to think, plan, and reflect.
  - o Turn off your car radio.
  - o Turn off your computer.
  - o Go for a walk.
  - o Spend some quiet time in nature.
  - o Use your "chillax zone" to get off that treadmill.
- Spend more of your conversation time listening than speaking.
  - o Listen, really listen, to yourself and others.
  - o Focus on all communication cues, not just the words.
- Slow down to speed up.
  - o Stop and listen to what others are telling you.
  - o Be open to and reflect on input from other sources.
  - o Let problems and ideas "marinate" in a resting mind.

7. QUIT STRIVING FOR SUCCESS . . . AND SEEK SIGNIFICANCE

- Our relationships are a primary source of purpose and significance in our lives. Ask yourself each day:

  o How do I define success?

  o What will I do today to create significance in my life?

- Look for ways to invest your three T's—time, talent, and treasure—in other people.

- Live in your sweet spot by answering these questions:

  o What am I absolutely passionate about?

  o Which tasks am I really good at?

FOUR MORE WAYS
TO
KEEP QUITTING…AND WINNING!

1. *Winners Always Quit* PowerPoint® Presentation

Put your team in the winner's circle! Introduce *Winners Always Quit* to your team with this complete, cost-effective companion piece. All the main concepts and ideas in the book are reinforced in this professionally designed, 62-slide downloadable presentation. It even includes speaking notes to make it a turnkey presentation for you! Use the presentation for kickoff meetings, training sessions, brown bag lunches, or as a follow-up development tool. **$99.95**

2. Keynote Presentation

Invite one of the authors to help your team quit the good things so they can stick to the great things. Lee and David both deliver practical, powerful tools participants can put to work right away. For more information, visit www.CornerStoneLeadership.com

3. Workshop

Facilitated by one of the authors or a certified facilitator, this half-day, fast-paced workshop will reinforce the principles of *Winners Always Quit* and bring to life the simple tools for swapping pretty good habits for really great results. Participants will create personal plans for quitting and winning!

4. *Winners Always Quit* self-assessment

Take this free, online questionnaire. A five-minute investment gives you a real-time, personalized feedback report to help you quit today and win tomorrow. Visit www.WinnersAlwaysQuit.net. Complimentary.

888-789-LEAD   www.CornerStoneLeadership.com

THE 𝒩ATURE OF ℰXCELLENCE
GIFT BOOKS & CALENDAR

Stunning photography and inspirational quotes are combined in *The Nature of Excellence,* a beautiful, 88-page gift book. Learn from the wisdom of more than 100 successful people who have inspired excellence throughout history.

Take a virtual tour of this elegant book at www.CornerStoneLeadership.com.

10 ½" x 10 ½" Premier Edition: $29.95 each
6" x 6" Classic Edition: $15.95 each (Available June 2009)

Customize this book for your team!
Call 888-789-5323 for pricing.

The Nature of Excellence Daily Inspiration includes an important attribute of excellence and a meaningful quotation. Perfect for office desks, school and home countertops. A great gift or motivational reward. $15.95

Accelerate Personal Growth Package
$159.95

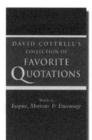
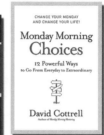

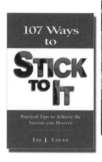

Visit www.**CornerStoneLeadership**.com for additional books and resources.

YES! Please send me extra copies of *Winners Always Quit!*
1–30 copies $14.95   31–100 copies $13.95   101+ copies $12.95

Winners Always Quit	_____ copies X _____	= $_____

Winners Always Quit Companion Resources
PowerPoint® Presentation (downloadable)   _____ copy X $99.95   = $_____

Additional Personal Growth Resources
Accelerate Personal Growth Package   _____ pack(s) X $159.95   = $_____
   (Includes one each of all items pictured
   on previous page)

Nature of Excellence Products
10 ½" x 10 ½" Premier Edition Gift Book   _____ copies X $29.95   = $_____
6" x 6" Classic Edition Gift Book   _____ copies X $15.95   = $_____
The Nature of Excellence Daily Inspiration   _____ copies X $15.95   = $_____

Other Books
_____   _____ copies X _____   = $_____
_____   _____ copies X _____   = $_____
_____   _____ copies X _____   = $_____

Shipping & Handling $_____
Subtotal $_____
Sales Tax (8.25%-TX Only) $_____
Total (U.S. Dollars Only)   **$**_____

Shipping and Handling Charges

Total $ Amount	Up to $50	$51-$99	$100-$249	$250-$1199	$1200-$3000	$3000+
Charge	$7	$9	$16	$30	$80	$125

Name _____ Job Title _____

Organization _____ Phone _____

Shipping Address _____ Fax _____

Billing Address _____ Email _____
                                  (required when ordering PowerPoint Presentation)

City_____ State _____ Zip _____

❑ Please invoice (Orders over $200) Purchase Order Number (if applicable) _____

Charge Your Order: ❑ MasterCard   ❑ Visa   ❑ American Express

Credit Card Number _____ Exp. Date _____

Signature _____

❑ Check Enclosed (Payable to: CornerStone Leadership)

Mail
Phone 888.789.5323   **P.O. Box 764087**
Fax 972.274.2884   www.**CornerStoneLeadership**.com   **Dallas, TX 75376**

Thank you for reading *Winners Always Quit*!
We hope it has assisted you in your quest for
personal and professional growth.

CornerStone Leadership is committed to providing new
and enlightening products to organizations worldwide.
Our mission is to fuel knowledge with practical resources
that will accelerate your team's productivity,
success and job satisfaction!

Best wishes for your continued success.

CornerStone
Leadership Institute

www.CornerStoneLeadership.com

*Start a crusade in your organization –
have the courage to learn, the vision to lead,
and the passion to share.*

✓ **YES! Please send me extra copies of** *Winners Always Quit!*
1-30 copies $14.95   31-99 copies $13.95   100+ copies $12.95

Winners Always Quit	____ copies X _____	= $ _____	

Winners Always Quit **Companion Resources**
PowerPoint® Presentation (downloadable)   ____ copy X $99.95   = $ _____

Additional Personal Growth Resources
Accelerate Personal Growth Package   ____ pack(s) X $159.95   = $ _____
(Includes all items shown inside.)

Nature of Excellence Products
10 ½" x 10 ½" Premier Edition Gift Book   ____ copies X $29.95   = $ _____
6" x 6" Classic Edition Gift Book   ____ copies X $15.95   = $ _____
The Nature of Excellence Daily Inspiration   ____ copies X $15.95   = $ _____

Other Books
_____   ____ copies X _____   = $ _____
_____   ____ copies X _____   = $ _____
_____   ____ copies X _____   = $ _____

Shipping & Handling $ _____
Subtotal $ _____
Sales Tax (8.25%-TX Only) $ _____
Total (U.S. Dollars Only)   **$ _____**

Shipping and Handling Charges

Total $ Amount	Up to $49	$50-$99	$100-$249	$250-$1199	$1200-$2999	$3000+
Charge	$7	$9	$16	$30	$80	$125

Name _____ Job Title _____

Organization _____ Phone _____

Shipping Address _____ Fax _____

Billing Address _____ E-mail _____
(required when ordering PowerPoint® Presentation)
City _____ State _____ ZIP _____

❏ Please invoice (Orders over $200) Purchase Order Number (if applicable) _____

Charge Your Order: ❏ MasterCard   ❏ Visa   ❏ American Express

Credit Card Number _____ Exp. Date _____

Signature _____

❏ Check Enclosed (Payable to: CornerStone Leadership)

Fax 972.274.2884
Phone 888.789.5323   www.**CornerStoneLeadership**.com   **P.O. Box 764087**
Dallas, TX 75376

wth Package $159.95

Becoming the Obvious Choice is a roadmap showing each employee how they can maintain their motivation, develop their hidden talents and become the best. **$9.95**

Getting it Together teaches you the EDGE process, a proven system that will assist you in decreasing stress while becoming more productive and getting things done faster. **$14.95**

175 Ways to Get More Done in Less Time has 175 really good suggestions that will help you get things done faster...and usually better. **$9.95**

Silver Bullets offers straightforward tips that will inspire personal and professional growth to take you to the top. **$14.95**

Conquering Adversity – Six Strategies to Move You and Your Team Through Tough Times is a practical guide to help people and organizations deal with the unexpected and move forward through adversity. **$14.95**

The Ant and the Elephant is a different kind of book for a different kind of leader! A great story that teaches that we must lead ourselves before we can expect to be an effective leader of others. **$12.95**

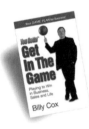

You Gotta Get In The Game...Playing to Win in Business, Sports and Life provides direction on how to get into and win the game of life and business. **$14.95**

Too Many Emails contains dozens of tips and techniques to increase your email effectiveness and efficiency. **$9.95**

One of each of the items shown here are included in the *Accelerate Personal Growth* Package!

Shift to Professional Paradise: 5 Steps to Less Stress, More Energy & Remarkable Results at Work is entertaining and fun to read, emphasizing personal accountability and the value of employee engagement across all industries. Real workplace stories and examples paint visual pictures, cement the concepts and promote long-term behavior change. **$14.95**

Do It Right! The New Book of Business Etiquette Take these tips on business trips, to meetings, interviews and presentations. Read *Do It Right!* today, and watch your career take giant steps forward! **$14.95**

Orchestrating Attitude translates the abstract into the actionable. It cuts through the clutter to deliver inspiration and application so you can orchestrate your attitude...and your success. **$9.95**

107 Ways to Stick to It What's the REAL secret to success? Learn the secrets from the world's highest achievers. These practical tips and inspiring stories will help you stick to it and WIN! **$9.95**

The Nature of Excellence Daily Inspiration is a compelling collection of quotes about leadership and life, is perfect for office desks, school and home. Offering a daily dose of inspiration, this terrific calendar makes the perfect gift or motivational reward. **$15.95**

Monday Morning Choices is about success – how to achieve it, keep it and enjoy it – by making better choices. Hardcover **$19.95**

David Cottrell's Collection of Favorite Quotations is compiled to reinforce the principles of *12 Choices...That Lead to Your Success*. Each quote was selected to inspire, motivate, and encourage you. **$14.95**

136 Effective Presentation Tips will take you step-by-step through a proven process of preparing and delivering a presentation that will get your point across to anyone, anywhere, anytime. **$9.95**

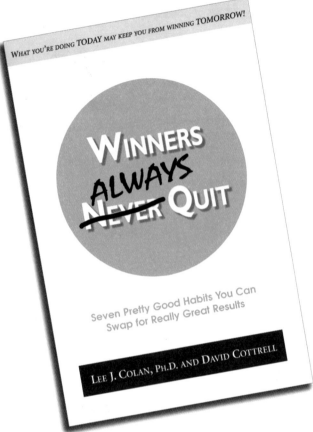

WHAT YOU'RE DOING TODAY MAY KEEP YOU FROM WINNING TOMORROW!

WINNERS
ALWAYS
NEVER QUIT

Seven Pretty Good Habits You Can Swap for Really Great Results

LEE J. COLAN, PH.D. AND DAVID COTTRELL

3 Easy Ways to Order Copies for Your Management Team!

1. **Complete the order form on back and fax to 972-274-2884**

2. **Visit www.CornerStoneLeadership.com**

3. **Call 1-888-789-LEAD (5323)**

CornerStone
Leadership Institute